Show M

Famous Missourians

Alice Anna Reese

Activities by: Heinrich Leonhard,
Ara Kaye, and Aimee Leonhard

Activities by Heinrich Leonhard
Additional contributions by Ara Kaye, and Aimee Leonhard

Ribbon map courtesy of
the State Historical Society of Missouri

Author photograph by Anastasia Pottinger

Published by Compass Flower Press
an imprint of AKA-Publishing

ISBN 978-1-936688-50-0

Show Me Famous Missourians

Written by Alice Anna Reese

with

Activities by: Heinrich Leonhard,
Ara Kaye, and Aimee Leonhard

Additional support from the
State Historical Society of Missouri

Acknowledgments

The creators wish to thank the State Historical Society of Missouri http://shs.umsystem.edu for their patience. Both retired State Historical Society employees Laurel Boeckman and Ara Kaye made important contributions.

We would also like to thank Stevan Reese for his technical assistance.

With heartfelt thanks, the author acknowledges the value of Write/Hear, the Columbia chapter of the Society of Children's Book Writers and Illustrators. This critique group, especially Claire Garden, have significantly improved these biographies.

Table of Contents

iii

Foreword

When I was a youngster of nine or ten, there was no television, no internet, and movies were an extravagance to a family with limited income. I was never without entertainment and I built friendships on a daily basis. I visited with kings and queens, with explorers and soldiers, with ball players and musicians, with movie stars and ministers. They came to my house in books—free—from the public library. Each night, I would gain a new friend on the printed page.

I had friends named Peter Rabbit and Babe Ruth, Abe Lincoln and Robert E. Lee, George Washington and Thomas Jefferson, Al Jolson and Roy Acuff. I knew them all. And don't forget Tom Sawyer, Huck Finn, Jim and Becky Thatcher. Each night, I would read myself to sleep and dream of my friend for the evening.

I was pleasantly surprised to meet some of my old friends in *Show Me Famous Missourians.* I renewed acquaintance with Jesse James, Mark Twain, Calamity Jane, George Washington Carver, Belle Starr, the Gingham Dog and the Calico Cat, and one of my first baseball heroes—Leroy "Satchel" Paige. I met Walt Disney in this new book—the cartoonist who gave me my first trip to the movies. I'll never forget *Snow White and the Seven Dwarfs.* Our meetings this time around were even better than the first—for I had a chance to play a game with each.

I enjoyed the challenge of being a fourth grader again, making new friendships and renewing old ones. There is nothing as rewarding as a book. A friendship made there lasts forever! Thank you, Alice Anna Reese and staff, for giving today's youngsters a chance to establish and enjoy a relationship with twenty famous—and infamous—Missourians.

By Bill Clark—A curmudgeon who owns no computer and still makes friends daily on the printed page.

Sacred Sun (1809?-1843?)

Portrait of Sacred Sun

We know her as Sacred Sun. Her name in the Osage language is Mohongo. Her portrait was painted in 1830 by Charles Bird King for the Washington D.C. Gallery of Indian Portraits. How that happened is an interesting story.

The first Osages visited France in 1725. Among them was Little Chief's grandfather. He met the French king Louis XV and spent three weeks touring France. Little Chief heard this story when he was a toddler. Legend has it that he cried out, "I also will visit France, if the Master of Life permits me to become a man."

The Osages began stockpiling furs to pay for Little Chief's trip to France when Sacred Sun was fourteen. The men hunted and trapped. The women prepared the skins. Twenty-five tribe members planned to cross the "Big Lake." But four years passed and some were not able to go. Little Chief, Sacred Sun, and ten other Osages loaded a raft with furs to for pay their passage and as gifts for the French king. Near St. Louis, the raft overturned. Everything was swallowed up by the river. The Osages swam to shore, then walked to St. Louis.

There the Osages met an old friend, a Frenchman named David Delaunay. He offered to take them to France with him. It seems that the Osages and Delaunay agreed that appearances by natives from the wilds of America would bring money and gifts to cover the cost of their passage. Delaunay asked an interpreter, Paul Loise, to go along. Half the Osages decided crossing the sea meant drowning and being eaten by fish. They turned back. But six—Little Chief, his wife Hawk Woman, her cousin Sacred Sun, Sacred Sun's husband Black Bird, a young warrior, and Big Soldier—decided to go on.

Eighteen-year-old Sacred Sun was pregnant. She may not have known it. Anyway, the Osages were young and on a lark. In New Orleans, they met a missionary they had known back in Osage country. He sailed for France days before the Osages and alerted the French press that exotic American Indians would soon be arriving. When Sacred Sun and her party anchored at Le Havre at noon on July 27, 1827, French newspapers had already spread the news. Thousands of curious onlookers swarmed the docks, some even hanging from the masts of nearby boats.

People wanted to touch the Osages' coppery gold skin. Sacred Sun, like Hawk Woman, painted a red line down the part between her braids. It represented the path of grandfather sun. The French were entranced. The Osages were wined and dined by the aristocracy. Newspapers carried daily stories of their activities. In honor of their audience with King Charles X, Little Chief painted red and blue stripes on his face, the colors of the French flag. The king treated them with fatherly affection. Then, on September 1, a notice ran in the newspaper saying "tickets would have to be secured to see the Osages either in the halls where they were to appear or in their apartments."

Sadly, interest in the Osages was already fading. Delaunay was arrested for some old debts and declared a swindler. Sacred Sun was now far along in her pregnancy. She wanted to go home. In Frankfurt, Germany, four Osages were forced to be exhibited up on pool tables in a bar. A newspaper recorded that Sacred Sun and Hawk Woman wept.

On February 10, 1828, in Liege, Belgium, Sacred Sun gave birth to healthy twin girls. Liege church women helped the young mother. One twin, Maria Elizabeth Josepha Julia Carola, stayed with Sacred Sun. A wealthy Liege woman adopted Maria Theresa Ludovica Clementina Black Bird. Unfortunately, that baby died within the year.

Meanwhile, the Osages back in Missouri were worried. Indian agent Hamtramck wrote, "Their relations are numerous and begin to grow noisy and troublesome, daily visiting me to know what has become of their friends...they have even gone so far as to threaten my life if their friends do not return soon...."

3

In an effort to find a way home, the Osages divided into two groups. Sacred Sun and the baby, her husband, and the young warrior went back to Paris. There they found the Marquis de Lafayette, French hero of the American Revolutionary War. He helped raise funds and arranged for a ship. But at the dock, their baggage was taken in payment for debts that had been secured in their names. Tragically, Sacred Sun's husband and the young warrior died of smallpox on the return voyage, leaving Sacred Sun with her baby to fend for herself.

The ship docked at Norfolk, Virginia. Superintendent of the Bureau of Indian Affairs, Thomas McKenney, took care of the young widow and her baby while she waited for her friends to arrive. McKenney asked Congress to pay Charles Bird King twenty dollars to paint Sacred Sun and her child so that he would have an Osage portrait for his Indian Gallery.

Meanwhile, the rest of the group, Little Chief, Hawk Woman, and Big Soldier traveled to southern France to the estate of Bishop Dubourg, whom they had known back in Missouri. Like Lafayette, Bishop Dubourg raised the money for their return trip.

On May 6, 1830, Sacred Sun and the baby, Little Chief, and their exhausted friends left Washington D.C. by stagecoach for St. Louis. Later, Lafayette sent them the luggage that had been seized at Le Havre.

Sacred Sun was among the last generation of her people to live a traditional life in the Osage tribal homeland in

Missouri. She was last seen on the Neosho River in 1833. Not long afterward the tribe was moved to Oklahoma.

Between 1821 and 1830, Charles Bird King painted over one hundred portraits of Indian visitors to Washington D.C. The portraits hung in a special gallery in the new Smithsonian Institution building. McKenney wanted to make a book. The portraits were shipped to Philadelphia. Henry Inman painted copies in oil. Black and white lithographs were hand colored from Inman's copies. Fire raged through the Smithsonian's second floor gallery on April 27, 1842, destroying most of Charles Bird King's Indian portraits, including the original of Sacred Sun. But the image of Sacred Sun is preserved in McKenney and Hall's *History of the Indian Tribes of North America* that was issued as a series between 1836 and 1844.

Decorate your teepee.

Kit Carson (1809-1868)

A Thoroughly Nice Guy

Kit Carson is famous as a trapper, as John C. Fremont's guide to the untamed West, and as an advocate for Native Americans.

Christopher Houston "Kit" Carson was one of sixteen children, the second child of his father's second wife. Kit was born in a log cabin on Christmas Eve, 1809. He was two months premature. A year later the family left Kentucky. Kit's mother rode horseback, Kit in her arms. They settled in Boonslick, near the Missouri River. While some of the settlers farmed, others patrolled, guarding against Indians. Yet Kit played with Indian children. Early on, he learned that some Indians were hostile and some were friendly. When Kit was eight, a burning branch fell on his father and killed him. Ten children were still at home. Kit needed to help his mother. As he later said, "I jumped to my rifle and threw down my spelling book. And there it lies." He became an accomplished horseman and hunter, but never did learn to read or write.

Kit was always at odds with his stepfather. So at age fourteen Kit was apprenticed to David Workman, a saddlemaker in the village of Franklin, Missouri. Meanwhile, three of Kit's older brothers followed the Santa Fe Trail west through the Rocky Mountains in what was then Mexican territory. For two years Kit sat at a bench mending harnesses and cutting leather. He got tired of sitting still. In late August, 1826, he ran away.

Mr. Workman sympathized (he would go west himself within a year), but he was required by law to report his apprentice's absence. Workman waited a month, then placed an advertisement in the *Missouri Intelligencer* of October 6, 1826:

Notice is hereby given to all persons, that Christopher Carson, a boy about 16 years old, small of his age, but thick-set; light hair, ran away from the subscriber, living in Franklin, Howard County, Missouri, to whom he had been bound to learn the saddler's trade, on or about the first of September last. All persons are notified not to harbor, support or assist said boy under penalty of law. One cent reward will be given to any person who will bring back said boy.

Kit had joined a caravan bound for Santa Fe as a "cavvy boy," a herdsman for the horses and oxen that were taken along as replacements for those that died along the trail. From Santa Fe, Kit made his way to Taos, home to the mountain men. He joined his first beaver trapping expedition when he was nineteen. It was a hard life. Besides grizzly bears and hostile Indians, there was freezing weather, thirst, and starvation.

In the spring of 1834, Kit and three friends were trapping the headwaters of the Laramie River. One afternoon Kit shot an elk on a ridge about a mile from camp. Grrrrr. Kit whirled around. Two grizzlies were loping toward him. No time to reload. Kit dropped his flintlock and shimmied up the nearest tree. One bear left, but the other one started pulling up nearby trees. Kit said he was never so scared in his whole life. As night was falling, the bear finally wandered off. When Kit was positive both bears were gone, he raced for camp. He didn't stop for the elk.

By 1842 beaver were becoming scarce and fashion was changing. Silk top hats were in, beaver hats were out. Kit Carson took a steamboat back to Missouri. On that trip he met John C. Fremont. Fremont was planning an expedition to map the western half of the newly opened Oregon Trail. He needed a guide. Kit said he had been in the mountains and could probably take Fremont anywhere he wanted to go.

Kit was only five foot four, shorter than average, probably because of his premature birth. But he was 135 pounds of solid muscle. He had a soft voice and keen blue eyes. Although he was illiterate, he spoke Spanish well enough to be an interpreter, and he had a working vocabulary of Apache, Arapaho, Blackfoot, Cheyenne, Comanche, Crow, Navaho, Paiute, Shoshone, and Ute. He also knew the universal Indian sign language.

Fremont was in the mountains east of Los Angeles when two Mexicans—an old man and an eleven-year-old boy—wandered into his camp. They had been guarding a herd of thirty horses when they were attacked by Paiutes. Two other men and two women had been herding the horses with them. While the four hid, the old man and the boy took the horses to a spring, but the Paiutes followed them and stole the horses. They had walked about thirty miles to Fremont's camp. Would Fremont help them recover their horses? Kit and another mountain man, Alex Godey, offered to help the Mexicans.

Kit and Alex trailed the Paiutes all day. Late that night they unsaddled their horses and wrapped themselves in sweat-soaked saddle blankets. They did not make a fire for fear of being seen. At dawn, the two men crawled into the Paiute camp. When a horse spooked, Kit and Alex leapt to their feet firing their pistols. Two Indians were killed. The others fled in panic. Alex, an arrow through his shirt collar, scalped both Indians. They rounded up the horses, drove them back to camp and returned them to the grateful old man. Later, Kit and Alex found the bodies of the four missing Mexicans. They had been tortured and killed.

Fremont's reports were published by Congress. Ten thousand copies were printed. It became the pioneer's guidebook for the Oregon Trail. It also made Kit Carson a national hero. Kit was appointed Indian agent for the Utes by the government in 1853. He was to make sure they had adequate supplies and were punished for raiding. Unlike many Indian agents, Kit was impeccably honest. He spent every penny the government sent on food and blankets for his Indian charges. Watching an Indian woman and child trudge barefoot through the snow, Kit realized the depth of the Indians' despair. As European Americans spread west into Native American ancestral lands, the hunting grounds were swallowed up. The Indians had nothing. No wonder many became thieves.

Kit Carson is the most famous of the mountain men. In his lifetime he traveled everywhere in the West. He became thoroughly sympathetic to the plight of the Native Americans. And, most unusual of all, everyone—European Americans, Mexicans, and Native Americans—liked him. He was a thoroughly nice guy.

▶ How to make rope:

- Tie two three-foot strings to a chair leg and a pencil.

- Twist about one hundred times while keeping a little tension on the string.

- Hold the middle of the twisted rope and move the pencil to the chair, let go of the middle, and watch it curl up.

- Straighten out the rope keeping the pencil next to the chair.

- Cut the string from the chair and tie a knot at the cut end.

12

Mark Twain (1835-1910)
The Adventures of Mark Twain

"I was born," Mark Twain wrote in his autobiography, "the 30th of November, 1835, in the almost invisible village of Florida, Monroe County, Missouri." Halley's Comet was blazing across the sky, its head large and brilliant white, its misty tail long and glorious. It would come again when Mark Twain died seventy-five years later.

America's most famous writer was named Samuel Langhorne Clemens at birth. He was two months early and sickly. Later his mother, Jane Clemens, was asked if she was afraid he would die. She paused, then said no, she was afraid he would live. Mrs. Clemens was fascinated by patent medicines and folk remedies. She hovered over Sam for four years in Florida and ten more after the family moved to Hannibal. When he was nine, Twain later recalled, "Mother used to stand me up naked in the backyard every morning and throw buckets of cold water on me.... And then, when the dousing was over, she would wrap me up in a sheet wet with ice water and then wrap blankets around that and put me into bed." Aunt Polly used the same cure in *Tom Sawyer*.

One of Sam's playmates in Hannibal was Tom Blankenship. He was "ignorant, unwashed, insufficiently fed; but he had as good a heart as ever any boy had." Sam liked him, but was forbidden to play with him, which, of course, made his society all the more desirable. Tom Blankenship became a model for Huck Finn. Missouri had been a slave state, so the fictional friendship between Huck and Jim, a runaway slave, caused a sensation.

When Sam was eleven his father died. Sam, with his mop of curly red hair and mischievous ways, was always playing hooky. Mrs. Clemens decided he needed to learn a trade. Joseph Ament edited the *Missouri Courier* in a room over the drugstore. At thirteen Sam went to work for Ament as printer's devil (apprentice printer). He swept the floor, ran errands, and restacked type. On cold mornings he built the fire. Year round, he brought water from the village pump. He washed down the rollers, washed the forms, folded the papers and delivered them at dawn Thursday mornings. Sam's pay was supposed to be meals, a sleeping pallet on the office floor, and two suits of clothes. His first suit fitted like a circus tent. There was no second. His pay did not include money.

That year, the year Sam turned thirteen, he found a torn page blowing in the street. It was about Joan of Arc's prison days in the Middle Ages. He researched her life, the life of a hero and a martyr. Later he wrote a satirical story based on those incredible events, *Personal Recollections of Joan of Arc by the Sieur Louis de Conte.*

As he read about the Middle Ages, Twain mused about the difficulties a knight could face. Armor would get red hot in the sun, leak in the rain, and freeze in the winter. It might be struck by lightning. The knight wouldn't be able to dress or undress. How would he scratch when he had lice? If he fell off his horse, how would he get back up? It was like being sealed in a tin can. How did a knight blow his nose or manage certain requirements of nature? After lots of research Mark Twain wrote *A Connecticut Yankee in King Arthur's Court* and *The Prince and the Pauper.*

Sam read all the time. After reading Lieutenant William Lewis Herndon's account of his exploration of the Amazon, twenty-one-year-old Sam decided to go to Brazil to make his fortune. He took the steamer *Paul Jones* down the Mississippi River to New Orleans, only to find that there would be no ships going to South America for at least a year. Sam returned to the *Paul Jones* and begged Horace Bixby, the boat's pilot, to teach him the pilot's trade. Back in Hannibal, all the boys had dreamed of working on steamboats, and being a pilot was the best, most respected, most revered job of all. Bixby agreed to take Sam on as his "cub."

Sam thought it would be easy—you just had to keep the boat in the middle of the big river. Wrong! Sam had to learn every town, island, and bend, every snag, sandbar, reef, shoal, and woodpile. He had to know where they were day or night, in sun or fog, going upstream to St. Louis or down to New Orleans. Bixby made Sam write everything down in a notebook. Within eighteen months, Sam had learned what he could about the twelve hundred miles of the constantly changing Mississippi River. *Life on the Mississippi* is a partly autobiographical, partly factual, thoroughly delightful book. It is said to be the first book submitted to a publisher in typewritten form.

When the Civil War broke out, commercial traffic on the Mississippi River stopped. Sam was out of the best job he would ever have (he didn't think writing was work). He was a soldier in the Confederate Army for a week, but he did not like the idea of being shot at. He tried silver and gold mining in Nevada for about a year. It was in a mining camp that he heard the jumping frog story. He recorded it, then rewrote it a half dozen times trying to get the humor right. "The Celebrated Jumping Frog of Calaveras County" was sent to a friend in New York who sent it on to a publisher. It was Sam's first published story, and it was reprinted in newspapers around the country and became an instant classic.

When he was not swinging his pick and ax searching for the mother lode, Sam wrote humorous letters to the Virginia City *Territorial Enterprise*. A wonderful, funny book, *Roughing It*, tells of his year mining. Sam failed at mining and was flat broke when a letter came offering him a job with the *Enterprise*. He tucked his pant legs into his boots and walked the 130 miles to Virginia City in order to accept the job. His serious reporting was signed Sam Clemens, but his humorous sketches he signed Mark Twain. It was a pilot term. When the leadman on a steamboat shouted "mark twain," it meant the river was two fathoms deep (twelve feet) and safe for passage.

Twain worked for various newspapers for a couple of years. The *San Francisco Chronicle* sent him on a cruise to Europe and the Holy Land. The letters he sent back to the paper became the basis of the satirical book, *The Innocents Abroad*. Those two books, *The Innocents Abroad* and *Roughing It*, made Twain famous.

For forty-five years, Mark Twain, America's notable humorist, gave lectures and wrote novels, stories, essays, and sketches to international acclaim. Twain died seventy-four years, five months after he was born, when Halley's Comet was again visible in the sky.

▶ Ribbon Map

Mark Twain knew about ribbon maps. Ribbon maps are long and narrow like a hair ribbon. They were used by steamboat captains or pilots so they would know where they were on the river and what towns and landings lay ahead. The map was unrolled from the top or bottom to show the trip upriver (against the current) or downriver (with the current).

Each map has a "legend" which tells about the map: the title, date, map maker, and publisher. Any special features are also noted in the legend.

The Coloney & Fairchild's *Ribbon Map of the Father of Waters*, published in St. Louis in 1866, is nearly eleven feet long and two inches wide. It unrolls from a wooden cylinder and shows the Mississippi River from Minnesota to the Gulf of Mexico. It can be seen at the State Historical Society of Missouri.

Make your own Mississippi River ribbon map from the images shown on the following pages. The four sections are for the Missouri portion of the Mississippi River.

To assemble your map, cut along the dotted lines to separate the parts. Each section has a number from one to four. Tape the parts together in order by number. Roll up the map and it is ready to use.

If you were the captain or pilot of a steamboat, you would unroll the map to the section of the river where your boat was located and let the ends roll out of the way. As the boat progressed down the river, you would unroll the map bit by bit to keep track of your location.

—Ara Kaye,
State Historical Society of Missouri
Ribbon map courtesy of the State Historical Society of Missouri

▶ Assemble your ribbon map:

Using the following illustrations, cut out each strip of the map. Tape section 1 of the map at the bottom onto the top of section 2 at the arrow where the image will overlap a duplicated illustration.

Section 1

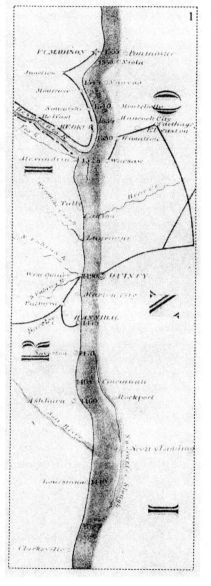

Section 2

Piece section 2 onto section 3 at the arrow, then section three onto section 4 at the arrow.

Section 3

Section 4

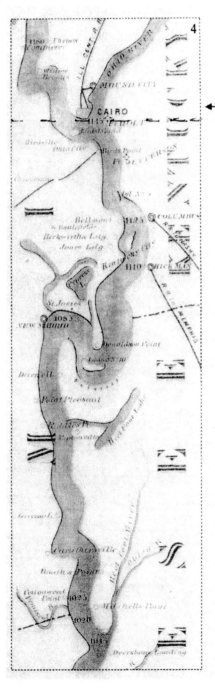

Jesse James (1847-1882)
The Dashing Outlaw

Jesse James was five feet, eleven inches tall, with alert blue eyes and a neatly trimmed beard. He never said anything he didn't mean. He didn't smoke or drink or swear. He was devoted to his wife and two children. Like his late father, Jesse wanted to be a preacher.

Missouri was admitted to the Union in 1820 as a slave state. The people of Kansas would vote to determine whether they would be a slave state or a free state. The people of Missouri thought their neighbor Kansas would become a slave state, but then abolitionists from New England began to settle in Kansas. From 1856 to 1865, Missouri pro-slavery bushwhackers and Kansas anti-slavery jayhawkers fought a vicious Border War.

William Quantrill had formed a guerrilla army that supported the South behind the front lines of the Civil War. His gang members were Missouri bushwhackers. Jesse's older brother Frank joined Quantrill's gang when he was nineteen. Their mother was a fiery, six-foot redhead. Though no official record of the following story exists, hanging a man to get information was common in those days. There are several versions of the events that took place in the spring of 1863. This is Jesse's mother's version.

Jesse's stepfather, Dr. Samuel, was out in the front yard. A group of Union soldiers rode up looking for Frank. Dr. Samuel said he didn't know where Frank was, so the men hung him from a tree to make him tell. Jesse's mother was watching from inside their log cabin. The Union men rode around to the back, where fifteen-year-old Jesse was plowing. They beat him with ropes as he ran through the cornfield. Meanwhile, Jesse's mother rushed out front and lifted her husband down. He was still breathing. A little while later Jesse limped in from the field, his back covered in blood. Mrs. Samuel nursed her husband and her son back to health. For the rest of his life, Dr. Samuel had difficulty speaking. Jesse wanted revenge. He rode off to join the bushwhackers.

Jesse recognized Brantley Bond, one of the men who had hung his stepfather. Bond had served with Frank in the State Guard, but now had joined the Union forces. A year passed. Then Jesse and a group of bushwhackers cornered Brantley Bond at his home. Jesse said, "Pray if you ever prayed in your life, because you've only got about a minute to live," then shot him dead.

Nearly all the inhabitants of Centralia were Northern sympathizers. The night of September 26, 1864, Bloody Bill Anderson and 225 men, including seventeen-year-old Jesse, camped out at the Singleton farm, four miles south of Centralia. Early the next morning Bloody Bill Anderson and thirty of his men rode into town. Frank James was with him but not Jesse. All of the Northern sympathizers were shot dead. The bushwhackers were ready to return to the farm at noon when a train arrived with twenty-two unarmed Union soldiers aboard. Anderson lined them up and shot them pointblank.

That afternoon, Major A.V.E. Johnston and three hundred mounted Union infantry rode into Centralia. When he heard what had happened, Major Johnston and a group of his men rode out to the Singleton farm. Arriving, he ordered his men to dismount and load their rifles. The bushwhackers could not believe their eyes. They jumped on their horses and rushed the Union men.

According to James family lore, Jesse "galloped to within five feet of [Major Johnston] and shot him through the brain." Over one hundred Union soldiers were killed. The bushwhackers lost three.

At the close of the Civil War, Missouri adopted the Drake Constitution. Those who sympathized with the Confederate cause could not teach school, preach the gospel, or run a business of any kind, however small. Many men returned to farming. The work was backbreaking. Jesse had no desire to farm, and he could not become a preacher. The economy was in recession. Thousands became outlaws. Jesse James rode the finest horses and could shoot a wild turkey through the eye. He became a bandit.

Jesse and Frank James robbed the Daviess County Savings Bank at Gallatin, Missouri, on December 7, 1869. Entering the bank, Frank laid a one hundred dollar bill in front of Capt. John W. Sheets, owner of the bank, and asked him to change it. Jesse entered. He thought Sheets was S.P. Cox, the man who had beheaded Bloody Bill Anderson. Bill was Jesse's friend. Jesse shot Sheets in cold blood.

The bank clerk ran into the street shouting that Capt. Sheets was murdered. As Jesse and Frank fled the bank, the townsmen opened fire. Jesse's horse shied, tangling Jesse's foot in the stirrup. He was dragged several feet, finally got free, and leapt up behind Frank. Later, the people of Gallatin identified the abandoned horse as Jesse's. The James brothers became wanted men.

One afternoon Jesse stopped at a rundown farm. The woman was alone, the widow of a Confederate soldier. After dinner Jesse paid her, as was his custom. The poor widow broke down. She told Jesse the bank was going to repossess her farm. Jesse asked when the banker was coming, what route he would take, and how much the mortgage was. It was several hundred dollars. Jesse had money from a recent robbery. He gave the widow the money she needed and helped her write a receipt for the banker to sign.

The banker arrived in the afternoon thinking he would soon own the farm. To his surprise, the widow paid the full amount and insisted he sign a receipt. Three miles down the road, our favorite outlaw jumped from the bushes and demanded the banker's money. Homer Croy, who did extensive research on Jesse James, said there are so many versions of this story that it is likely that it actually happened.

The simple truth is that the law did not know what Jesse and Frank James looked like. And no one would help them. For sixteen years the James gang robbed trains and banks without disguises. It would not have been possible without the support of the local population. The banks were seen as greedy and the trains as corrupt. Farmers fed Jesse and his gang in their kitchens and hid them in their barns.

In the end, Jesse James was shot in the back of the head by a young member of his own gang. Six months later, Frank James handed his pistol to Missouri's governor. Neither brother was ever convicted of a single crime.

▶ **Make your own wanted poster:**

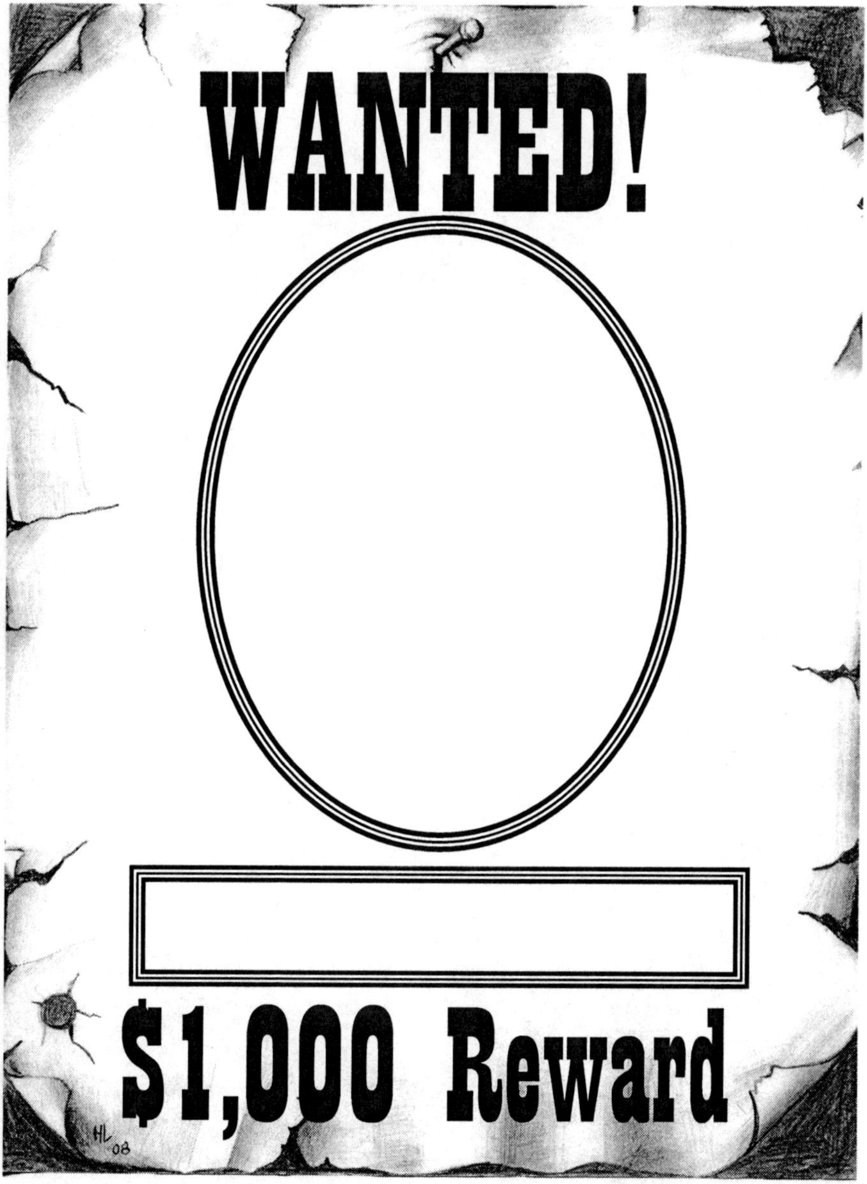
WANTED!
$1,000 Reward
HL 08

Belle Starr (1848-1889)
A Starr Among Thieves

Belle Starr was a lady—sort of. She dabbled in stealing horses and kept rough company, but she was well educated and a loyal friend. It's just that following the Civil War, most of her friends became outlaws. Two of her brothers and both of her husbands were shot and killed. So was Belle. Most of the stories connected with her are fiction, the product of the dime novels that were so popular at the end of the nineteenth century.

Myra Maybelle Shirley was born February 5, 1848, in Carthage, Missouri. Called May most of her life, she was the middle of seven children. All of the children were well educated. Her father, John Shirley, owned The Carthage Hotel and a tavern called The Shirley House. He kept a couple of slaves, and The Shirley House was a meeting place for Southern sympathizers. Jesse James, Cole Younger, Jim Reed, and other young men who fought for the South and later rode with outlaw bands, often stopped by.

John Shirley also had a library of good books. Before he moved to Missouri, he had been a prosperous farmer in

Kentucky and still kept a string of fine Kentucky racehorses. Belle's mother Eliza was a Hatfield of the famous Hatfield/ McCoy feuding families. Unlike her neighbors, Eliza affected the manners of a refined Southern lady.

May was small, dark, and pretty, with the Hatfield hair-trigger temper. Her best friend was her brother Bud. Six years older than May, Bud taught her to ride sidesaddle, as was proper for a lady, and to shoot both a pistol and a rifle. By the time she was ten years old, she was a skilled rider and a competent shot.

May attended the Carthage Female Academy. She was intelligent and mastered its curriculum of reading, spelling, grammar, arithmetic, manners, Greek, Latin, Hebrew, and music. She was a good pianist. When the Civil War began, the school closed and everything changed.

Bud was twenty-one when he joined William Quantrill's guerilla army to fight for the Confederacy. As May watched her beloved brother ride away, she swore to help the South any way she could.

The Richeys were known Union sympathizers. They lived in Newtonia, thirty-five miles from Carthage. Fifteen-year-old May rode up to their mansion late one evening in February 1863. She claimed she had been visiting friends and gotten lost. Mr. Richey invited her to join them for supper and to spend the night. The other house guests included Major Eno and his Union officers. Their troops were using the

Richey's stone barn and mill as barracks. After supper, May played the piano for the family and their guests. The next morning Belle had her horse saddled and brought to the door before breakfast. Saying she must hurry because her parents would be concerned, she cut several switches for her horse from the cherry bush beside the house. The switches were a signal. The number cut told the watching bushwhackers the size of the Union force. After May rode away, the house was attacked by Quantrill's gang and destroyed.

When Bud was killed by Union soldiers, John Shirley, saddened by his son's death and by business losses, packed up two Conestoga wagons and moved his family to Texas. Jim Reed and May had been friends in Missouri. When Jim's family settled in Texas not far from the Shirleys, romance bloomed. May was eighteen and Jim twenty when they were married by the Reverend S. M. Wilkins on November 1, 1866. Like so many Civil War veterans, Jim had difficulty settling down to farm. He turned to stealing horses and gambling at the races. May did not approve. After all, they had two small children. They had been married eight years when Jim was killed trying to escape arrest. After his death, May bought a livery stable.

May's late husband had been taking the stolen horses to Tom Starr, a notorious Cherokee outlaw who lived in Indian Territory, outside of U.S. jurisdiction. May married Tom's tall, handsome son Sam in a Cherokee ceremony. Only then did she drop May and become Belle Starr. Sam, Belle, and her children lived in a log cabin in a remote valley of the Cherokee Nation. The house was on a loop of the South Canadian River called Younger's Bend. The Younger brothers had hidden out there so often, old Tom Starr had named it for them. Belle loved it there.

There is only one crime we know for certain that Belle committed. She and Sam were arrested September 21, 1882, for stealing Andrew Pleasant Crane's horse, valued at eighty dollars. They were taken to jail. When Belle and Sam appeared before a jury, Sam claimed he was in bed with the measles at the time of the theft, and Belle said that a man named Childs had the stolen mare. Unfortunately, someone said they had seen Belle riding the horse. The couple was convicted and ordered before Isaac Parker, the famous hanging judge, for sentencing. (Parker had sent eighty-eight men to the gallows to be hung.) He sentenced the Starrs to one year in the Detroit House of Corrections.

Belle charmed the prison guard and ended up giving music lessons to his children. Meanwhile, Sam slaved away breaking rocks with a sledgehammer. Both of them were released for good behavior after nine months.

Belle never forgot her genteel Southern upbringing. On occasion she dressed in a black velvet riding habit. With her dark tan and long black hair, she was often mistaken for an

Indian. She had small feet, was vain about them, and wore very expensive boots. Her beautiful "Belle Starr" sidesaddle was richly carved. When riding alone out in the country, she buckled on a Colt .45 that she called "my baby."

Belle's hat blew off as she was riding across the prairie near Fort Smith. A cowboy named William Kayser was approaching. Belle told him to retrieve her hat. He refused. Belle drew her pistol and ordered him to pick it up. Without hesitating, Kayser retrieved the hat and handed it to her. Belle cautioned him, "Next time do what a lady asks."

On February 3, 1889, three years after Sam had been killed in a brawl, Belle was ambushed and killed. There were several suspects. One was her son. Belle had whipped him. A neighbor she had argued with was brought to trial, but the case was dismissed for lack of evidence. Belle's flash temper had made her lots of enemies.

▶ Barn Star

You will need a square sheet of paper and a pair of scissors. A mountain fold makes a tent. A valley fold is the opposite, it makes a ditch.

1. Fold the paper in half to form a rectangle.
2. Fold the lower right corner up and across, placing it 1/3 to 1/4 of the way from the top left corner.
3. Fold the lower left corner over the edge you just folded across.
4. Fold the flap on the right to the opposite edge.
5. Cut diagonally from just below the middle of the right edge to the left corner.
6. Unfold star.
7. Fold the five long folds into mountain folds and the five short folds into valley folds.

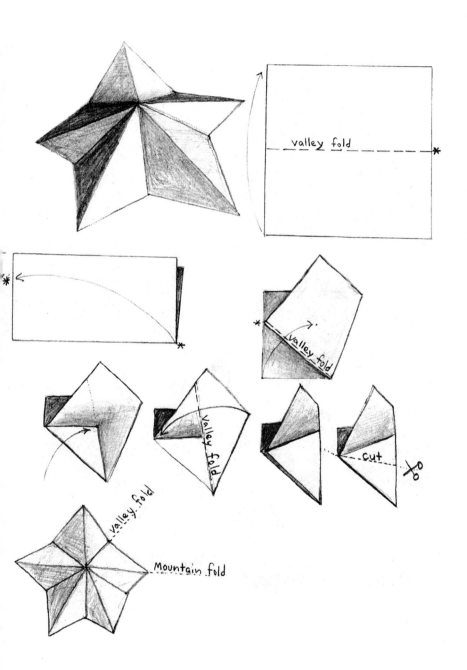

valley fold

valley fold

valley fold

valley fold

cut

valley fold

Mountain fold

Eugene Field (1850-1895)
A Citizen of Cloud Country

Eugene Field was a brilliant newspaperman. He was famous in his time both as a humor columnist and as "The Children's Poet." His best known poems are "Wynken, Blynken, and Nod" and "The Gingham Dog and the Calico Cat."

Born in St. Louis, Missouri, Eugene Field was four months old when a twelve-year-old Irish girl was given complete charge of him. Temperance Moon fed the mischievous Eugene a diet of leprechauns and fairies. She raced through the house with him and made him little sugar pies.

When Eugene was six years old his mother died of cholera. Of her eight children, only Eugene and his younger brother Roswell had survived. The boys were sent to live with their aunt in New England. Their cousin, Mary Field French, a thirty-year-old single woman, took charge of their education. For the most part, Eugene was a poor student; but he did correspond with his father in Latin.

Cousin Mary gave the boys freedom to roam the hills and woods. Eugene loved flowers, and he always had one or two animals in his pocket: a chipmunk, a baby rabbit, a couple of grasshoppers, a lizard, or the mole that lived in a bureau drawer. It seemed he could tame anything. All his animal friends had names and, according to Eugene, each spoke a different dialect of English. Luckily, Eugene was able to converse with each of them. Even the chickens seemed to answer to their names.

Eugene was a newspaperman all of his adult life. The final twelve years he worked for the *Chicago Daily News*. His column, "Sharps and Flats," appeared in the morning edition and dealt with the goings on about town. His humor was wicked. No one was immune to his biting satire, but he was never mean or bitter. His famous poetry also found an audience in his newspaper column. Much of it was inspired by the delightful mob of eight children produced by him and his adored wife.

Eugene Field was well over six feet, but he stooped. He was incorrigibly cheerful. He had big, deep-set, china-blue eyes, a face with a deathly pallor, and a thin glow of hair. Mornings he played with the children. About eleven o'clock he arrived at the office wearing one of his gaudy neckties. First thing, he took off his shoes and rolled his trouser legs halfway to his knees. Then he put on slippers with crushed heel counters, so the slippers flapped when he walked. At his desk he rolled up his shirtsleeves, unbuttoned his waistcoat, unbuttoned his suspenders, and removed his collar. Slumping onto his chair, he crossed his legs over the desk corner, slippers dangling from his toes.

The first hour or two he horsed around with his friends, then went out for dinner. He didn't settle into writing until about three in the afternoon. With a pad of paper on his lap, he wrote diligently for three hours. His tiny writing was neat and easy to read. If anyone made a noise or disturbed him while he was writing, he had a big tin plate above his chair that he would hammer.

Eugene had an old linen office coat. When he discovered colored inks, he wrote his column in a variety of colors. Rather than change pens when he changed colors, he just cleaned his pen on his coat. On warm days the coat hung on a hook near his desk. Even then, he used it as a pen wiper.

The silent partner in Field's column was a little fox terrier named Jessie. She was white with yellow ears and a brownish blaze over her left eye. Her identifying mark was the absence of a nail on her left forepaw. It had been lost to one of the family hens. (The hens were named Finniken, Minniken, Dump, Poog, and Boog.) Jessie climbed in Eugene's lap and napped while he wrote. Eugene read his poems to her. It was important that she agree. Jessie always wagged her stump of a tail approvingly, and, according to Field, "smiled her flatteries as only a very intelligent little dog can."

Using material from his newspaper columns, Field published several volumes of satire, prose, and poetry. The poem that made him famous was "Little Boy Blue." It is not the one we are familiar with, but a sad poem that may refer to Field's first son, who died when only a few months old. "Little Boy Blue" was set to music. It was read in schools. Even as far away as the Shetland Islands, where seashells were the only toys and children sucked on dry fish instead of candy, the children recited Field's "Little Boy Blue."

That international success led Field to consider writing lullabies for children around the world. "Cornish Lullaby," "Norse Lullaby," even "Japanese Lullaby" can be found in his columns. One of his most famous poems, the Dutch lullaby "Wynken, Blynken, and Nod," was first written on brown wrapping paper. It appeared in Field's "Sharps and Flats" newspaper column March 11, 1889.

Field said, "I am deeply interested in folklore and fairy tales. I believe in ghosts, in witches, and in fairies." He passionately believed that tales of giants, ogres, witches, and fairies were essential to children's health. According to Field, modern children (he was speaking of children in the late 1800s) were too concerned with getting *things*.

Eugene was also full of pranks. One time, to get a pay raise from the editor of the *Chicago Daily News*, he dressed four of his children in rags. Standing before the editor like beggars, they stretched out their hands and raised appealing eyes to his face. Field begged, "Please, sir, won't you raise my salary?" His plea was granted promptly.

In spite of being a famous children's poet, Field confessed that he didn't love all children (although children were always crawling up on his lap). He said, "I have tried to analyse my feelings toward children, and I think I discover that I love them insofar as I can make pets of them." He said that if he had had a fairy godmother, he would have wished for a big astronomical telescope and a Twenty-four-tune music box. Eugene was as cheerful as a pocket gopher with full cheek pouches. His head was safely tucked in the clouds. Eugene Field squeezed as much happiness out of life as he possibly could.

▶ **Color the picture of the Gingham Dog and the Calico Cat.**

HL
08

THE DUEL

The gingham dog and the calico cat
Side by side on the table sat;
'Twas half-past twelve, and (what do you think!)
Nor one nor t'other had slept a wink!
The old Dutch clock and the Chinese plate
Appeared to know as sure as fate
There was going to be a terrible spat.
(I wasn't there; I simply state
What was told me by the Chinese plate!)

The gingham dog went "Bow-wow-wow!"
And the calico cat replied "Mee-ow!"
The air was littered, an hour or so,
With bits of gingham and calico,
While the old Dutch clock in the chimney-place
Up with its hands before its face,
For it always dreaded a family row!
(Now mind: I'm only telling you
What the old Dutch clock declares is true!)

The Chinese plate looked very blue,
And wailed, "Oh dear! what shall we do!"
But the gingham dog and the calico cat
Wallowed this way and tumbled that,
Employing every tooth and claw
In the awfulest way you ever saw—
And, Oh! How the gingham and calico flew!
(Don't fancy I exaggerate!
I got my news from the Chinese plate!)

Next morning, where the two had sat
They found no trace of dog or cat;
And some folks think unto this day
That burglars stole that pair away!
But the truth about the cat and pup
Is this: they ate each other up!
Now what do you really think of that!
(The old Dutch clock it told me so,
And that is how I came to know.)

~*Eugene Field*

Calamity Jane (1856-1903)
Tall Tales of the West

Telling tall tales was a campfire talent that Calamity Jane had. Since records are scarce and Calamity Jane was illiterate, the truth about her life is difficult to piece together. She did, however, dictate an autobiography in 1896. Much of it is wishful thinking (she never was a scout, never killed any Indians, never traveled with General George Armstrong Custer), but many stories, especially from her childhood, are at least partly true.

There is no birth record for Martha Canary, Calamity Jane's birth name. Marthy, as she was called, does appear in an 1860 census record. At that time she was four years old and living in a two-story log house on a backwoods farm near Princeton, Missouri. Her father, Robert Canary, was a fairly successful farmer. Her mother, Charlotte, wore bright-colored clothes, drank, cursed, and smoked cigars. According to the local rumor mill, Robert had found her in a bawdy house and hoped to reform her. Marthy was the oldest of their six children. She loved the outdoors and spent most of her time riding horses. She says she got so good, she could ride the most vicious, most stubborn horses. It is unlikely she ever went to school. When her father was accused of stealing, he sold the farm and left Missouri with six-year-old Marthy and the family.

Gold was discovered in Alder Gulch, Montana in 1863. Hoping to get rich, the Canary family joined a wagon train to Virginia City, Montana. On the trail, Marthy spent most of her time riding and hunting with the men. It was quite an adventure. Sometimes the way was too rough for the horses. Then the wagons were lowered over ledges with handheld ropes. Sometimes streams were flooded because of heavy rains or wagon wheels got stuck in quicksand or boggy places. In her autobiography Marthy says, "Myself on more than one occasion have mounted my pony and swam across the stream several times merely to amuse myself and have had many narrow escapes from having both myself and pony washed away to certain death." They were five months on the trail. "By the time we reached Virginia City," Marthy recorded, "I was considered a remarkable good shot and a fearless rider for a girl of my age."

The winter of 1864-1865 was especially hard and cold in Virginia City. Supply trains often didn't make it through, and the price of food soared. A newspaper article in the *Virginia City Daily News*, dated December 31, 1864, tells of three little girls by the name of Canary knocking on the door of James Fergus and asking for help. Commissioner Fergus worked for Madison County and was in charge of aiding the poor. Marthy was carrying her baby sister. The little girls were dressed in thin calico slips. Mrs. Fergus gave the children food and clothing, and the girls returned to Nevada City, a mining camp nearby.

The family moved from mining camp to mining camp. In the spring of 1866, the children's mother died in Blackfoot City, Montana. The next year in Salt Lake City, their father died. Marthy was eleven. All the children were probably put in homes for adoption, but soon Marthy was out on her own. First she went to Fort Bridger in Wyoming Territory. She lived in Mrs. Ed Alton's boarding house and babysat for her. When Mrs. Alton learned Martha was seen at a dance wearing some soldier's uniform, Martha was fired. It was a pattern that would repeat itself throughout her life.

Martha Canary disappeared in 1870 and reappeared as Calamity Jane in about 1875. No one knows how she got her nickname, although there are lots of stories. What is known is that wild girls were often called "Calamity Jane," but for Martha Canary the name stuck.

No place is more closely associated with Calamity Jane than the Black Hills of South Dakota. Miners had flooded into the Indian lands when gold was discovered. In order to determine the extent of the mineral resources, the government formed an expedition headed by geologist Walter P. Jenney. Four hundred soldiers commanded by Lieutenant Colonel Richard Irving Dodge accompanied them. Wearing a soldier's uniform, nineteen-year-old Martha tagged along. She did the soldiers' laundry, mended their clothes, and took care of them when they were sick.

Off and on for years Calamity Jane worked as a bullwhacker. Bullwhackers walked beside the long teams of oxen that pulled the lines of freight wagons carrying anything from railroad ties to baskets of potatoes. Trail work was slow and monotonous. Calamity Jane became adept at picking a fly off the ear of an ox with a twenty foot whip and cursing a blue streak.

Twenty-one-year-old Calamity Jane joined Wild Bill Hickok's party to return to the Black Hills. In Deadwood, she immediately went to work as a dancehall girl. Dancing with the girls did not cost anything. But when the dance was over the men escorted the girls to the bar for a drink. The owner split the profits from the liquor sales with the girls.

White Eye Anderson was a cook with the Hickok outfit. He told this story: TidBit was a redhead from Salt Lake City. Like Calamity Jane she had come to Deadwood with the Hickok party. She had "entertained" Laughing Sam, who ran a poker game. Instead of paying her with gold dust as he promised, Laughing Sam had given TidBit brass filings mixed with black sand. When Calamity Jane found out, she grabbed her boyfriend's two ivory handled six-shooters and headed for the saloon. Waving the guns in Sam's face, Calamity Jane cussed him out for cheating her friend, then she forced him to give TidBit two twenty dollar gold pieces.

In New York in 1877, Ned Webster began a thirty-three issue Deadwood Dick series of dime novels with Calamity Jane as the cursing, cigar-smoking heroine. Dime novels in those days were like television and Facebook today. Martha went from being a local novelty to a national legend. Although she said the dime novels were full of lies, people assumed she was like Wild Bill Hickok and Buffalo Bill. So she made up a history for herself. She had been a scout, rescued stage coaches, etc., etc.

There's no question there was a real Calamity Jane. She was a flamboyant, drinkin', cussin', cigar-smokin', pistol-totin' fireball. But most of the stories about her aren't true.

The wagon master or leader of a wagon train headed west published the following list of supplies that each family should have ready to take with them. The trains usually departed in early April so they could reach their destination in time to build cabins and plant before winter set in.

Suggested provisions:

~A good strong wagon that can carry at least two thousand pounds

~Good double cover for the wagon.

~3 yokes of oxen between four and seven years old. Oxen should be broken to the yoke before departure.

~200 pounds of flour per person over ten. One Hundred pounds per each child between three and ten years of age.

~15 pounds of coffee and fifteen pounds of sugar per person.

~1,000 pounds of bacon per person over ten. Five hundred pounds for each person between three and ten.

~50 pounds of salt per family.

~60 pounds of rice and six pounds of pepper per family.

~50 pounds of dried fruit, apples, and peaches.

~3-5 bushels of corn meal.

~A tent large enough for five to eight persons.

~Each man should be armed with a good rifle or heavy shotgun with five pounds of powder and fifteen pounds of shot.

Modern-day provisions:

▶ What do you need today if you were going on a trip lasting six months?

_____

_____

_____

_____

_____

_____

_____

_____

_____

_____

George Washington Carver
(1865?-1943)
A Flower in His Lapel

To George Washington Carver, science and religion were inseparable. "Nature in its varied forms are the little windows through which God permits me to commune with Him." Of his research Carver said, "The primary idea in all of my work was to help the farmer and fill the poor man's empty dinner pail." Known as "The Peanut Wizard," George Washington Carver changed the South, its farming practices, and its farmers forever.

Moses Carver was a white man who raised horses in Diamond Grove, Missouri. He had built a snug one room cabin for his wife, Susan. Their baby girl had died, and Susan was lonely. Moses did not believe in slavery and would not have a field hand for himself. But he bought thirteen-year-old Mary for seven hundred dollars to keep Susan company. Mary fell in love with Giles, a neighbor slave, and had five children. George was a baby when Giles, his father was accidentally killed.

Toward the end of the Civil War, members of the Ku Klux Klan turned to slave raiding—stealing slaves to sell in the Deep South. The day before Christmas in 1865, masked men rode into the Carver farm. Moses hid Mary's two-year-old Jim in the woods, but the raiders found Mary and her baby in Mary's little log cabin. Christmas morning Moses rode to town leading his finest racehorse. He thought John Bentley might know where the bushwhackers had taken Mary. Moses gave Bentley the horse to trade for Mary and offered him a forty acre woodlot if he could bring her back. Bentley rode off before noon.

On a cold, rainy afternoon six days later, Bentley appeared carrying a ragged bundle under his coat. He wasn't sure whether the baby was alive or dead. George had gotten whooping cough, and the kidnappers had left the worthless bundle with some women down near Conway. Bentley trailed the bushwhackers halfway through Arkansas trying to find Mary, but lost them in hill country. He handed the half dead baby to Moses. Passing the child to Susan, a grateful Moses told Bentley to keep the racehorse.

Uncle Moses and Aunt Susan, as the boys called them, brought the brothers into their little cabin and raised them as their own children. Jim helped Moses with the field work. George, always frail and sickly, helped Susan in the house and garden. When his chores were finished, George played in the woods, transplanting wildflowers to his secret garden. He was always asking questions. "I wanted to know every strange stone, flower, insect, bird, or beast. No one could tell me." He decided he would have to go to school.

The Carvers taught the boys to read from Aunt Susan's old copy of Webster's *Elementary Spelling Book*. A school for white children was nearby. Although the Civil War had freed the slaves, it was illegal for black and white children to attend the same school. Lincoln School for Colored Children was eight miles away. Aunt Susan packed a dinner for George to eat on his long walk to Neosho. School was over by the time he arrived. He found a barn nearby and curled up in the hay. Luckily, the barn belonged to a childless black couple, Mariah and Andrew Watkins. They agreed to help him go to school if he helped Aunt Mariah with the laundry she took in. She taught George to identify medicinal herbs. George went to church with her. Mariah gave him a Bible for Christmas. He read it every day until the day he died. Aunt Mariah said, "That boy told me he came to Neosho to find out what made hail and snow, and whether a person could change the color of a flower by changing the seed. Imagine!" Before long, George realized he knew more than his schoolteacher, and he moved on.

For the next ten years, George moved around the Midwest. He went to school and supported himself doing laundry and cooking. He graduated from high school in Minneapolis,

Kansas. At Iowa's Simpson College he studied art. When his teacher, Miss Etta Budd, found out that George loved plants, she suggested he study botany at Iowa State University where her father taught horticulture.

Aunt Mariah had encouraged George to help their people. Maybe, George thought, God's plan was for him to study agriculture. He enrolled at Iowa State. When he graduated, Miss Budd handed him a bouquet of red carnations. He stuck one in his lapel. He tucked a flower in his lapel every day after that.

Meanwhile, Booker T. Washington had started a college for black students in Alabama. Freed slaves needed economic independence. With a master's degree in plant science from the best agricultural college in the United States, George Washington Carver was the best qualified black agricultural scientist in the country. Washington persuaded him to join Tuskegee's faculty. Riding the train eight hundred miles south, Carver saw the deep black soils of Iowa change to the worn out red and yellow clays of Alabama. He watched listless black farmers pick endless rows of cotton.

At Tuskegee, Carver wore rumpled suits with a fresh flower in his lapel. It wasn't Iowa State. There was no laboratory. Carver and his students rummaged through the dump. Glass bottles were formed into beakers. An old ink bottle with a piece of string through a cork became a Bunsen burner. Nothing was wasted.

"For recreation," Carver once said, "I go out and hoe, pull weeds, and set plants myself." His students said he could make a nail bloom. It also seemed Carver could identify every plant and insect. The students decided to fool him. They took the head of a big ant and attached it to the body of a beetle with the legs from a spider. They had found it in a barn, they said. Could he identify it? Looking it over, Professor Carver replied that he believed it was a "humbug."

Carver issued bulletins and gave monthly lectures to local farmers. For those who could not come to Tuskegee, he loaded an old mule-drawn wagon with plants to show farmers the results of his research. He stayed in their shanties, ate their food (although he often brought along a bag of vegetables), and listened to their problems.

George Washington Carver never knew his parents. Birth records were not kept for slaves. He was a brilliant scientist and a devout Christian. He freed the South from its one-hundred-year dependence on cotton. He researched crops like peanuts and sweet potatoes and experimented with hundreds of uses for them. He showed that farmers could improve their families' diet by planting vegetable gardens. He demonstrated that worn out soils could be made fertile with readily available compost and manure. George Washington Carver worked every day of his life to make the world a better place.

▶ **Make words from** **P E A N U T**

1.		**17.**	
2.		**18.**	
3.		**19.**	
4.		**20.**	
5.		**21.**	
6.		**22.**	
7.		**23.**	
8.		**24.**	
9.		**25.**	
10.		**26.**	
11.		**27.**	
12.		**28.**	
13.		**29.**	
14.		**30.**	
15.		**31.**	
16.		**32.**	

Laura Ingalls Wilder (1867-1957)
Seeing with Words

Laura Ingalls Wilder was a pleasant, soft-spoken woman who didn't like crowds. When Laura was sixty-five, she published the first of her books for children, *Little House in the Big Woods*. It is the story of little Laura growing up in a snug log cabin surrounded by a loving family. Much to her surprise, the book was an instant success. During the next twelve years, seven more *Little House* books were published.

With young Laura, we experience the struggles and joys of pioneer life. Crops fail. Disease strikes. The winter of 1880 brings blizzard after blizzard and near starvation. The Ingalls family is hard-working and courageous. Pa plays his fiddle and the family sings—silly songs, romantic songs, hymns. It lightens the load. Laura's personal history is the history of America.

The oldest Ingalls child, Mary, was born in 1865. Laura was born two years later. A homebody, Mary loved studying. Laura loved milking the cow and caring for the calf. She loved being outdoors. She did not think she could ever soak up enough sunshine. The girls were best friends.

Mary was fourteen when she got a terrible fever. Ma cut off Mary's long, beautiful hair to keep her head cooler. For a time everyone thought she would die. After a while, the fever passed. Wrapped in quilts, week after week, she rocked in Ma's old hickory rocking chair. She began to get her strength back, but each day she could see less. One day, one awful day, Mary could not see the sun shining on her face. She was blind. Laura never forgot how patient and uncomplaining Mary was.

Laura was twelve at the time. Pa said Laura should be Mary's eyes. She must see out loud for Mary. When Mary was well again, she and Laura walked out on the prairie in the evening. Laura "saw out loud" for Mary: "The sun has gone through the white clouds. It is a huge, pulsing ball of liquid fire. The clouds above it are scarlet and crimson and gold and purple, and the great sweeps of cloud over the whole sky are burning flames." Making pictures with words became a habit for Laura.

Mary loved to study. Laura did not. Mary wanted to be a schoolteacher. Laura did not. To help Mary, Laura studied hard and did her lessons out loud so Mary would learn them, too. A family friend, Reverend Alden, told Pa about a college for the blind in Iowa. The college offered a seven year course of academic and manual arts training. Laura knew Mary wanted to go to the college.

One summer Pa worked construction in the brand new town of De Smet in the Dakota Territory. Mr. Clancy's dry goods store was one of the first buildings. Pa asked Laura if she would like to help sew shirts for his store. Laura did not like town, did not like being around strangers, did not like sewing. But she wanted to make money to help pay Mary's college tuition. For six weeks, Laura sewed buttonholes on men's shirts by hand. She wished there were more work. She wanted Mary to start college as soon as possible.

With the six dollars Laura made, the hundred dollars Pa made, and the sale of the corn and the oats on their land, Mary was able to start college that fall. Only when everything was settled did Laura realize how much she would miss Mary.

For a lot of children at the time, learning to read was education enough. But both Laura's mother and grandmother had been teachers. Laura passed the test to be a teacher before she was sixteen. When she was not teaching in tiny rural schools, she was back studying with her high school class. All her money went to help pay Mary's college fees.

Unasked, for three years Almanzo Wilder and his magnificent pair of Morgan horses collected Laura on Friday from her little schools so she could spend the weekends with her family. Laura's beautiful brown hair was so long she could sit on her braid. She did not encourage him at first, but she did like going out riding with him. Laura was eighteen when they married.

Laura and Almanzo drove their covered wagon from De Smet to the Land of the Big Red Apple in Missouri. Their daughter Rose was seven. They bought a farm near Mansfield in Missouri's Ozark Mountains. Almanzo built a house there for Laura. Today, the farm site and buildings are open to tourists.

The Wilders brought Laura's portable writing desk with them. Almanzo had made it for her. It was a wooden box polished shiny-smooth that opened out to be a slanted writing surface. At the top was a tray for Laura's pearl-handled pen with an inkwell next to it. Underneath there was a place for writing paper.

Laura began writing for the *Missouri Ruralist*, a local farm magazine. Her simple, sensible essays soon became regular features of the magazine. She saw women as equal partners on the farm and in the workplace. She loved farm life and was an authority on raising chickens. Unlike her neighbors, she could get her hens to lay eggs in winter.

When Laura was sixty, she bought stacks of orange-covered school tablets of lined paper from a Springfield grocer. Each tablet cost a nickel. Always thrifty, she wrote with a pencil from edge to edge on both sides of the paper. She filled the pages with stories of her childhood and put them in a big box. She asked some friends privately what they thought she should do with them. They said she must publish them.

Laura's daughter Rose typed the stories. She was a professional writer. She edited the stories and lectured her mother on theme and tone and point of view, then found a publisher for the books. Since then, Laura Ingalls Wilder's *Little House* books have been translated into dozens of languages. They have been read and enjoyed by millions of children all over the world.

▶ Diorama Directions

Solid lines are cut lines. Dashed lines are fold lines.

House

Cut out each piece along the solid lines. Color your house. Don't forget windows so the people inside can see out and doors so the children can go outside and play. Fold the tab on the dashed line and tape it to the other end of the house. Fold roof on the dashed line and tape it to the top of the house.

Farm

Line a shoe box or other small box with drawing paper. Draw the background for your farm diorama. You could include a barn, fences, fields, flowers, and farm animals. Place your house in your farm.

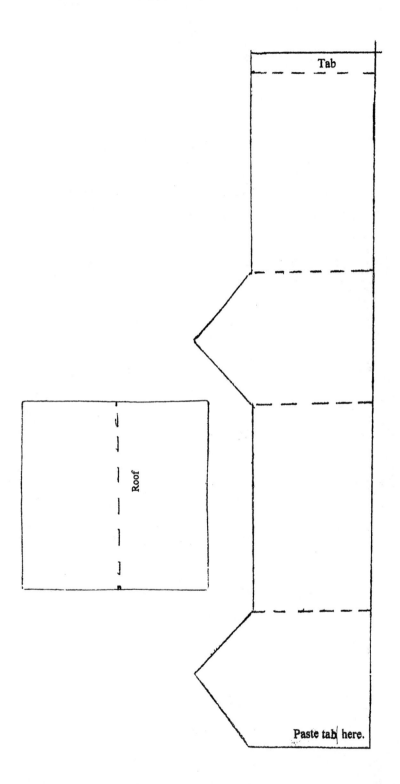

Tab

Roof

Paste tab here.

Trees

Color your trees. Cut one of each tree. Cut along solid line to the center of the tree. Slide the two parts together. Fold at the base of the trunk and tape your tree to the diorama.

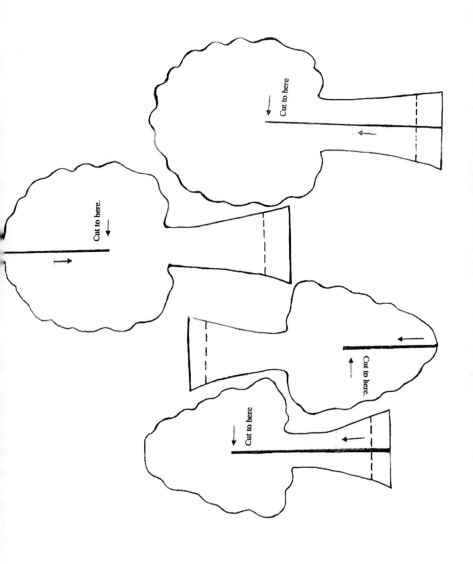

Cut to here

Cut to here.

Cut to here.

Cut to here

Carl Heinrich Boller (1868-1946) and Robert Otto Boller (1887-1962)
Fantasy Architects

Movies always provide an escape from the dull and humdrum. Early on, the architecture of movie theaters was a doorway into the happily-ever-after world where royalty reigned and life was beautiful. Carl and Robert Boller were master movie theater architects of the early twentieth century. They designed theaters from vaudeville to drive-ins. They specialized in ornate movie palaces.

Carl and Robert's parents immigrated from Germany. They married on July 4, 1865, in Brunswick, Missouri. The Bollers set up household in St. Joseph, Missouri, and had three sons and seven daughters. Will was firstborn and Carl was second. Nineteen years later, Robert was the last of the children.

Not a lot is known about them, but it appears that neither Carl nor Robert had any formal training in architecture. Their older brother Will worked in vaudeville, a music hall type of live entertainment. Will was "Boller the Magician" as well as a scenery painter. He traveled with a troupe in a circuit through Kansas and Missouri. In 1898, thirty-year-old Carl joined Will's troupe as another scenery artist.

According to family tradition, in 1903 Carl was working on scenery design in Pittsburg, Kansas. He was asked to help plan Pittsburg's new theater. He understood the architectural requirements for a vaudeville theater from practical experience. The LaBelle was the first theater Carl Boller designed. It was a three story brick building. The main floor had box seats along the walls and a large stage. There were three balconies. Tickets for seats in the "chicken roost," as the third balcony was called, were fifty cents. Carl's design included a projection booth, because five- and ten-minute silent moving pictures were just becoming available. The LaBelle burned in 1915.

The Louisiana Purchase Exposition, known as the St. Louis World's Fair, opened in 1904. Several European countries built pavilions in the fanciful styles popular in the Old Country. The variety and richness of these pavilions inspired the Midwest public and the architectural world. The exposition influenced many Boller theaters over the next several decades. The year following the fair, Carl moved his office from St. Joseph to Kansas City, Missouri.

Like Carl, Robert finished eighth grade at the Ernst School in St. Joseph, Missouri. Not only did neither brother study architecture, neither of them studied geometry. Robert loved live theater. He spent his allowance on performances at the local theaters and opera houses. After graduation, Robert worked for a series of St. Joseph companies before joining a carnival troupe. In the fall, eighteen-year-old Robert joined the firm of Carl Boller, Architect, as an apprentice draftsman.

Nevada was experiencing a gold rush in 1907. Boomtowns were springing up everywhere. Several of them hired Carl Boller to build nickelodeons, theater houses that charged a nickel to see moving pictures.

Robert Boller went to the West Coast to supervise architectural work for the Sullivan and Considine vaudeville circuit. Four years later, he was back working with his brother in Kansas City. The firm became a partnership—Carl Boller and Brother. The brothers joined the American Institute of Architects. The Kansas City chapter made Carl president in 1917.

Robert served in the United States Corps of Engineers during World War I. Carl, fifty years old, kept the business going from their office in Kansas City's Gayety Theater Building. When Robert returned, the firm was renamed Boller Brothers.

The Boller brothers had designed at least sixty-five theaters by 1919, establishing themselves as specialists in the architectural field of theater and movie palace design. Each theater was unique. Its design was influenced by the history of the town where it was located and the civic organization that funded it.

"Movie madness" swept the country in the 1920s. There was a huge boom in movie theaters. The brothers' work expanded rapidly. In 1920, Robert set up an office in Oklahoma. A year later he returned to run the Kansas City office so that Carl could move to California and open a branch office in Los Angeles. Carl Boller spent the rest of his career designing theaters for the western United States from his office in Los Angeles.

At least thirty-three Boller Brothers theaters are still open or undergoing restoration. At least fourteen are listed on the National Register of Historic Places. They include the KiMo Theater in Albuquerque, New Mexico, the Missouri Theater in St. Joseph, Missouri, and the Missouri Theatre Center for the Arts in Columbia, Missouri.

Built in 1927, the KiMo Theater in Albuquerque is filled with Indian designs and references to Indian culture. The white exterior stucco walls are intended to imitate a Pueblo adobe. Longhorn skulls with light-bulb eyes border the proscenium. The style of the Missouri Theater in St. Joseph is Mid-Eastern. The audience appears to be surrounded by the desert. A plaster tent-like canopy is tied to the walls by plaster ropes and shields the audience from an intense sky blue ceiling. The lavish interior is modeled on the palace ruins at Persepolis, capital of ancient Persia (known today as Iran). The jewel-like interior of the Missouri Theatre Center for the Arts in Columbia is an ornate blend of the Baroque and Rococo styles of the periods of the French kings Louis XIV and Louis XV. Workmen were brought from Europe and fixtures like chandeliers were ordered from established European houses.

The Boller brothers helped shape the emerging architectural form of the movie palace. They designed or consulted on the design and construction of more than 300 theaters in the Midwest and on the West Coast. Many have been demolished or modified, but fortunately, many have been restored to the elegance of the fantasy age of movie palaces.

▶ SHADOW PUPPETS:

Use your hands to make shadow puppets like these. Then make up your own!

James Cash Penney (1875-1971)
The Upside Down Company

At first J.C. Penney was in business to make money. Money was success. Then he realized that in order to expand his business he had to train good men to open more stores. Good men were success. Then he understood that happy customers were the real key to success. The J.C. Penney Company put customers served by well trained men above money. This was upside down from the way most companies were run in the early twentieth century.

On September 16, 1875 James Cash Penney was born on his father's farm two and a half miles outside of Hamilton, Missouri. Named after his father, he was the seventh of twelve children. Only six survived to become adults. Jim's father was a college graduate and Baptist preacher. Because preachers were not paid, Jim's father had a farm and raised cattle. Jim's mother had attended a convent school for Southern young ladies. She was a patient, gentle person. Jim's mother and father were cousins.

Jim had just turned eight. He was small for his age. There was the acrid smell of kerosene from the lamp in the Penney living room. His father's voice was firm and quiet. "Jim, you are going to have to buy your own clothes from now on."

Jim was startled. The soles of both his shoes had holes. "But Pa, won't you buy me just this one pair of shoes, then let me start in?"

"No, Jim. You'll have to figure out something. That's the way it'll have to be now."

Jim earned his first money helping his father with the haying. That $2.50 would buy a pair of shoes, but Jim decided to go into business. He went around to the neighbors asking if he could make a deal. He said, "If I can have your garbage, I'll wash up the buckets." Jim put cardboard in his shoes and bought a little black Berkshire pig. He built a pen for it and fattened it on the neighbors' garbage. He sold it and bought a pair of shoes and more pigs.

With more pigs, the neighbors' garbage was not enough. Jim found some scrap wood in the barn. He made horses from broomsticks that would scrape the ground. He painted them bright colors, some with stripes, some with zigzags. All had names. On Saturdays the neighborhood kids climbed on and raced the stick horses around the fields. They turned up heaps of weeds and grass. Jim had lots of feed for his pigs.

For two years Jim was in the pig business. But pigs are noisy animals at feeding time and smelly beasts in summer. The neighbors complained. Jim's father told him he would have to sell the pigs immediately. It was not fall, and the pigs were not close to market weight. Jim objected silently. He would not, could not, argue with his father. Neighbors are important. Jim sold his pigs the next day.

Jim never did well in school. "The main reason," he said, "was that, having to provide for my own clothing needs, it was too important to me planning how to make a dime."

Jim was nineteen and out of school. He helped on the farm, but he didn't like farming. His father had tuberculosis and was dying. But Mr. Penney hoisted himself out of his sickbed to go downtown to Hamilton's leading dry goods store. He asked J.M. Hale, owner of Hale's, to hire Jim. "Mr. Penney, to tell the truth I don't need another hand. February is a dull month. But I'd like to accommodate a son of yours. If the boy wants to learn the business while he makes himself generally useful, I'll give him twenty five dollars for the rest of the year." Even back then, a salary of $2.27 a month was almost nothing. But Jim was happy. He was sure he was meant to be a salesman.

Monday morning, February 4, 1895, Jim arrived early for work. "What can you sell?" asked Mr. Hale. "I can sell clothing," Jim replied brightly. But when one of his friends came into the store, Jim discovered that he could not sell his friend a suit. He did not know cotton from wool. He was embarrassed. He began to study the different fabrics. He learned the stock so thoroughly that he could close his eyes and tell grade, weight, and price by feel. The second year his salary was two hundred dollars. The third year Jim's health began to fail. Fearing tuberculosis, the doctor ordered him to a drier climate.

After a couple false starts, on March 29, 1899, Penney started work at the Golden Rule Store in Evanston, Wyoming. The owners, T.M. Callahan and Guy Johnson, took the golden rule seriously. They treated their customers fairly. And they had a novel idea—they wanted to form a chain of stores with partner/managers. When Penney married, he wanted to open his own Golden Rule Store.

Callahan and Johnson agreed Penney would open a store in Kemmerer, Wyoming, a town of around a thousand people, mostly sheep farmers and coal miners. Penney rented an empty building, one and a half stories with no plumbing and no electricity. The new Golden Rule Store opened at sunrise on Monday, April 14, 1902. It was midnight when Penney closed the store that first day. He trudged up the stairs with the day's earnings, mostly coins. He emptied the bag on a table in front of his wife. They had made $466.59! The people of Kemmerer took saving seriously. To save a penny for them, Penney recycled wrapping paper and saved short ends of string, empty boxes, and bent nails. Nothing was thrown away. He did not offer credit. He did not deliver. He offered quality goods at cheap prices.

Callahan and Johnson split up and sold Penney three of their stores. But Penney liked the partnership idea. He trained men to open new stores as partner/managers. Their primary responsibility was to train new men, creating a chain of partners. In 1909, Penney's Golden Rule Stores were incorporated as the J.C. Penney Company. It was, however, a unique type of corporation. Instead of public ownership, it belonged to the partners. J.C. Penney retired as president and became chairman of the board on January 1, 1917. It had been fifteen years since his first store had opened in Kemmerer. There were 127 J.C. Penney stores doing an annual business of more than eight million dollars. Penney was forty-one years old.

James Cash Penney took a frontier town dry goods store and expanded it based on the idea of good service and profit-sharing partnerships. But the J.C. Penney Company has changed. At this time there are about 1,090 stores, and the company is publicly owned.

▶ Color the stick horses

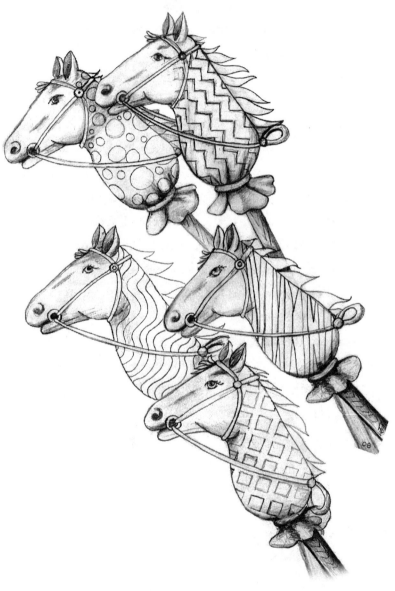

Harry S Truman (1884-1972)
One of Us

Of himself he said, "I'm just a common everyday man whose instincts are to be ornery."

Harry S Truman was born in Lamar, Missouri, on May 8, 1884. He was the first of three children. He was named Harry after his uncle, Harrison Young. But, you will notice, he wasn't named "Harrison;" he was given the diminutive "Harry" as a legal first name. The family decided he needed a second initial. His two grandfathers were named Anderson Shipp Truman and Solomon Young. Harry was given the middle initial S. It was understood that the S referred to both grandfathers. So, when he was sworn in as President of the United States, and the Honorable Harlan Stone, Chief Justice of the Supreme Court, began, "I, Harry Shipp Truman," Truman corrected him, "I, Harry S Truman."

Sitting on his mother's lap, Harry learned to read from the family Bible when he was four, but he was not able to read the fine print. The following year the family went to Grandview, Missouri, to celebrate the Fourth of July. The night ended with a spectacular fireworks display. Harry reacted to the sound of the fireworks, but he did not seem to see the colorful star clusters exploding overhead. Mrs. Truman was worried.

Mr. Truman, a horse and mule trader, was away on business, but Mrs. Truman decided Harry's eye problem was urgent. She hitched two horses to the farm wagon, planted Harry on the seat beside her, and drove fifteen miles to Kansas City. Dr. Thompson, the eye doctor, said Harry had flattened eyeballs. He prescribed thick glasses. Harry was wearing about the same prescription when he was president. In 1889, those double-strength, wire-rimmed spectacles were expensive. They cost ten dollars.

Harry's world was transformed. Because of the danger of his glasses breaking (they were made of glass, plastic hadn't been invented yet), he was forbidden rough-and-tumble play with the boys. Indoors, the cook taught him to make biscuits. (At one point he would make biscuits in the White House.) He and his little sister Mary Jane played duets on the piano. He braided her hair and sang her to sleep with lullabies. Harry admired his mother's caustic opinions about everything from windy preachers to crooked politicians. Like any farm child, he had chores. Mostly, though, he read books.

When Harry was six, the family moved into Independence so he could go to a town school. Harry loved reading biographies and history. For his tenth birthday Mrs. Truman gave him *Great Men and Famous Women*, a large four-volume set of books with titles in gold leaf. Harry considered it one of his life's turning points. He read them all. He especially liked the volumes entitled *Statesmen and Sages* and *Soldiers and Sailors*. These weren't children's books. The stories were reprints of articles from leading magazines, written by well-known authors. He also read Shakespeare and had read the Bible through twice before he turned twelve.

By 1944, Harry S Truman had been a banker and a farmer (the latter for twelve years), served in the army in World War I, co-owned a men's furnishings store that had failed, and worked his way up the political ladder to the U.S. Senate. He never did go to college.

Dissatisfied with Henry Wallace as vice president, the Democratic Party made Senator Truman the ailing Franklin Delano Roosevelt's fourth term vice president. Within three months of Inauguration Day, F.D.R. was dead. Truman was sworn in as President of the United States in the Cabinet Room of the White House.

After the ceremony, President Truman asked the Cabinet members to stay. With Truman at the head of the table, the Cabinet took their seats. The press secretary rushed in. The newspaper correspondents wanted to know if the San Francisco Conference to write the Charter for the United Nations would open as planned in twelve days. Truman, like F.D.R., hoped the new United Nations would help bring global peace after the century's two horrible World Wars. President Truman's answer was an emphatic yes—his first presidential decision.

It had been eighteen months since the Germans had surrendered. Negotiations to end World War II in Europe were already underway. President Truman went to Germany, to Potsdam on the outskirts of Berlin, to work out the details of the surrender with England's Prime Minister Winston Churchill and Russia's Generalissimo Joseph Stalin.

Meanwhile, the war with Japan raged on. About the time the Germans had surrendered, the Japanese high command had determined that they also were defeated, but they firmly believed in "death before dishonor." No Japanese military unit ever surrendered. They fought to the death. The United States planned to invade the Japanese home islands November 1, 1945. It was going to be bloody.

"Think of the kids that won't be killed! That's the important thing," was Truman's overwhelming reason for unleashing the atomic bomb. Secretary of State George Marshall had estimated that a quarter of a million American soldiers would be killed or seriously wounded in the invasion and an equal number of Japanese. No one close to the president was telling him not to use the bomb.

The first atomic bomb, a uranium bomb, was dropped on Hiroshima August 6, 1945. President Truman was on board the heavy cruiser USS *Augusta*, returning from Potsdam. The bomb leveled four square miles of the city. It killed eighty thousand people. Another sixty thousand would die by year's end of radiation poisoning and injuries suffered. The Japanese did not surrender. Three days later a second bomb, a plutonium bomb, was dropped on Nagasaki. The next day Emperor Hirohito said, "We must bear the unbearable." Japan surrendered.

As thirty-third president, Harry Truman faced history head on. He was a scrappy fighter, and those were difficult times. He would say, "My Missouri is the Missouri of Mark Twain and Jesse James." Former British Prime Minister Winston Churchill said to Harry Truman, "You, more than any other man, have saved Western civilization."

▶ Harry S Truman Word Search

Find these words in the word search. They run up and down, down and up, left to right, right to left, and diagonally. Some letters are used more than once.

Atomic Bomb	**Harry S Truman**	**Senator**
Banker	**Hiroshima**	**Stalin**
Cabinet	**Japan**	**United Nations**
Churchill	**Lamar Missouri**	**World War II**
Farmer	**Nagasaki**	
F.D.R.	**President**	

```
L  L  I  H  C  R  U  H  C  D  J  O  X  R  Y
H  A  R  R  Y  S  T  R  U  M  A  N  P  Z  U
E  T  M  M  O  R  Q  U  Y  L  P  G  X  O  N
O  O  N  A  G  A  S  A  K  I  A  I  G  N  I
R  M  N  T  R  A  Y  I  P  V  N  O  I  C  T
I  I  G  U  E  M  Z  V  O  K  G  L  H  A  E
I  C  P  Z  A  N  I  X  I  D  A  W  N  N  D
R  B  X  P  I  Q  I  S  F  T  N  A  M  V  N
A  O  Z  O  W  L  E  B  S  S  Q  S  R  Q  A
W  M  Y  R  Y  N  P  I  A  O  V  I  P  P  T
D  B  G  F  A  R  M  E  R  C  U  E  A  T  I
L  F  M  T  T  N  E  D  I  S  E  R  P  O  O
R  D  O  P  Z  A  M  I  H  S  O  R  I  H  N
O  R  U  R  L  L  U  W  Z  V  O  P  T  G  S
W  E  C  K  H  W  Q  B  A  N  K  E  R  G  O
```

Word Search by Ara Kaye

89

Harry S Truman Word Search

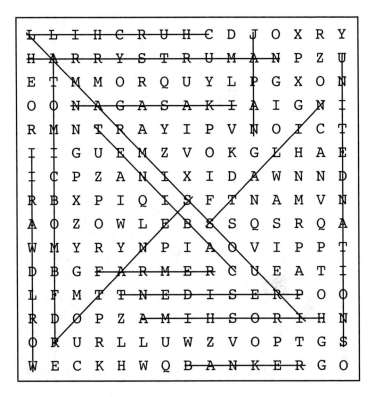

L L I H C R U H C D J O X R Y
H A R R Y S T R U M A N P Z U
E T M M O R Q U Y L P G X O N
O O N A G A S A K I A I G M I
R M N T R A Y I P V N O I C T
I I G U E M Z V O K G L H A E
I C P Z A N I X I D A W N N D
R B X P I Q L S F T N A M V N
A O Z O W L E B S S Q S R Q A
W M Y R Y N P I A O V I P P T
D B G F A R M E R C U E A T I
L F M T T N E D I S E R P O O
R D O P Z A M I H S O R I H N
O R U R L L U W Z V O P T G S
W E C K H W Q B A N K E R G O

Solution

Mary Paxton Keeley (1886-1986)
"I Was Born Liberated"

Mary Paxton Keeley believed that a writer's duty is to catch and preserve the life of her time in a net of words. Her father thought she was infected with *cacoethes scribendi*— the writing germ. Mary Paxton Keeley wrote ALL her life. She was Kansas City's first female reporter. Mary Paxton Keeley wrote books and magazine articles, essays, poetry, and plays. She was a journalism teacher in Columbia, Missouri, at Christian College (now Columbia College) for twenty-four years.

Mary Paxton Keeley was born into a house full of books in Independence, Missouri. When she was nine years old, a cousin in Virginia sent her a hood covered in feathers. Pete Allen was twelve years old. He and his gang of big boys always made fun of Mary when she wore it.

Mary, in her feathery hood, and her little sister Lib were walking to school one morning. Pete started yelling, "Kitty, Kitty, Kitty." All the other boys started yelling, "Kitty, Kitty, Kitty." Mary wanted to crawl into a hole. Lib pushed through the crowd of boys and trotted ahead. Mary tried to follow, but the boys blocked her way. She was scared. She was angry. She tried to think what to do. She thought about the kitten. The previous week the big boys had captured a mangy little kitten and had thrown rocks at it. The kitten fought back. She scratched the boys so hard, they let her go. Mary thought, I can fight back too.

Down the road Pete was balancing on the railing of a footbridge. "Kitty, Kitty, Kitty," he teased. His arms were spread wide, balancing him. Mary rushed at him. With her little pointer finger she pushed him backward off the bridge into the icy water. Mary looked down at him. His eyes were wide with surprise. Mary turned and ran all the way to school. The big boys did not bother her again, and they never let Pete forget how little Mary had made a fool of him.

Mary was twelve when her mother got sick with tuberculosis and had to stay in bed upstairs. Mary was the oldest, and her four brothers and sisters demanded jam for their bread. Mary became the jam maker. When the different kinds of berries, plums, peaches, pears, and apples were ripe, Mary's father hitched the old horse, Nellie, to the carriage and drove the children out to pick fruit. What the children did not eat, Mary made into jam.

Making enough jam to feed her siblings through the winter was not easy. But, there were twenty-seven children living on their block. Mary made big, cool pitchers of lemonade and told endless stories. Charmed, the neighbor children and Mary's little brothers helped her stem the strawberries and stone the cherries.

By September everything was ready. Mary took her father down into the cellar. The long shelves sagged under the weight of jellies and jams, and, of course, jar after jar of gooseberry jam, her father's favorite. When he said, "Well done, my dear, dear daughter," the hot summer's work was worth it.

Mary and her mother became close during the seven years of her mother's illness. Mary asked her mother if she was afraid. Her mother said, "No, I am not afraid. Death to me is just like going into the next room and shutting the door behind me, except, of course, I do not think I can ever open it again." She died when Mary was seventeen.

Mary always had a writing project going. She said, "You know when you have the writing germ: you're restless when you're not writing and irritated when you are because you think you're not doing as well as you want."

In the fall of 1907, Mary learned that the University of Missouri in Columbia was about to open America's first journalism school. She decided to enter. Mary Paxton was the first woman to graduate from the first school of journalism in the United States.

One week after graduation she was hired by the *Kansas City Post* as their first female reporter. She earned eight dollars a week. The U.S. Army announced it was testing a flying observation post. With it, enemy troop movements and artillery positions could be spotted from the air. It was a collection of giant kites. Mary volunteered to go up in it. Soon Mary was soaring several hundred feet above Kansas City, clutching the ropes. Her story of the adventure made the front page of the *Post* and created a sensation.

Mary married Edmund Keeley, a farmer, in 1919. They had a son, John Paxton Keeley. After seven years of marriage, Edmund Keeley died.

Mary returned to Columbia with her son. She got a master's degree and was offered a professorship at Christian College. She taught journalism and creative writing. It was, at that time, a genteel girls' school. Mary cut her hair short like a man, wore comfortable clothes and sturdy shoes, and rode her bicycle to work. She told her students they were not to call her Professor Keeley or Mrs. Keeley. They were to call her Mary Pax. She found, much to her surprise, that she liked teaching.

Wherever she went, Mary started a newspaper: on a boat she started the *Deck Swabber*; in Battle Creek, Michigan, the *Fumigator*; at Christian College she started the *Microphone*. Every Christian College freshman was required to write a play. After six years, Mary edited a collection of poetry from the *Microphone* and a book of prize-winning plays written by the girls.

Mary wrote *River Gold*, a children's book about pirates and buried treasure. She wrote and produced several plays at Christian College, including a three-act play about Vinnie Ream. Vinnie had attended Christian College and, when she was eighteen years old, had sculpted the statue of President Abraham Lincoln that stands in the U.S. Capitol Building.

Mary Paxton Keeley spent, on and off, seventy years writing. She said, "When they get me nicely settled in my coffin, I'll sit up and say, 'Oh, wait a minute, I have an idea.'"

▶ **Find these pictures of Missouri's state symbols.** They are hidden in the picture of Mary Paxton Keeley pushing Pete Allen off the bridge.

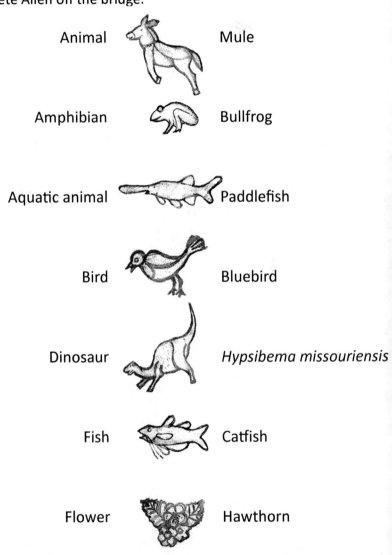

Animal — Mule

Amphibian — Bullfrog

Aquatic animal — Paddlefish

Bird — Bluebird

Dinosaur — *Hypsibema missouriensis*

Fish — Catfish

Flower — Hawthorn

Folk Dance Square dance

Fossil Crinoid

Grape Norton

Horse  Missouri fox trotter

Insect Honeybee

Mineral Galena

Musical Instrument  Fiddle

Tree  Dogwood

Thomas Hart Benton (1889-1975)
Maverick Muralist

Thomas Hart Benton was a cocky, storytelling kind of a guy with great talent and a wonderful sense of humor. A historical muralist and master of design, he is Missouri's most famous artist.

Thomas Hart Benton was born in Neosho, Missouri, into a family of lawyers and politicians. His father was a United States congressman. The granduncle he is named for was one of Missouri's first senators. As firstborn son, Tom was expected to follow the family tradition.

But Tom liked to draw. He liked to draw trains. He drew them on everything. The central staircase in the Benton house went around a landing between the lower hall and the second floor. Tom was about six when the house was redecorated. The stairway was papered a lovely creamy white. With a piece of charcoal, Tom drew a caboose at the bottom step. Mounting the winding stairs, boxcars followed flatbed cars. The long freight train was laboring heavily. The grade was steep. As the engine reached the second floor, it belched out great puffs of thick black smoke. Sadly, Tom's mother did not appreciate Tom's art. She lectured him, then removed his masterpiece with bread crumbs.

Later, young Tom would sit and look at a ripple of water and think about its texture and form, its colors. Or a rock. Or a bush. Or a fence post. He would stare at it for hours, forgetting what it was, immersing himself in what he was seeing. His mother decided he had talent.

At seventeen, Tom quit school. He got a job on a survey crew in Joplin. One Saturday night he was in the House of Lords, Joplin's fanciest saloon. Hanging over the bar was a large painting of a masked nude. Tom was short and young and was regarding the painting intently. Fellows at the other end of the bar laughed at him. Tom blushed. He said he was NOT staring at the naked woman, he was studying the artist's technique. One of the men asked if he was an artist. Benton replied, "Yes, by God, I am! And I'm a good one." He hadn't touched a pencil in months. He had never thought of himself as an artist.

The men took Tom down the street to the office of Joplin's new newspaper, the *Joplin American.* In a small room at the top of a narrow stairway, the editor steered Tom over to the window. "That's Jim Keena," he said, pointing across the street at the man behind the drugstore counter. "You go over there and draw Jim so we can recognize him and you are hired." Full of confidence, Tom borrowed pencil and paper, sketched the man, and landed himself a job as the *American*'s cartoonist.

The following February, Tom enrolled at the Chicago Art Institute. The moment he stuck his brush in a fat gob of color, he gave up newspaper cartooning. He was going to be a painter.

After a year at the Chicago Art Institute, Tom went to Paris to study the newest trends in art: impressionism, pointillism, cubism, and surrealism. Three years later he returned to New York. His paintings followed every "ism" that came along. It was several years before he realized that to be an artist in America, he needed an American style. He had to give up "jumping cubes...cockeyed tables, blue bowls, and bananas."

Murals became Tom Benton's favored art form. He said, "I like to do murals because I can put more stuff into them." And he was passionate about history—not the history of great men and glorious battles, but stories of the ordinary people who shaped America—the people's history.

Benton was invited to paint a mural in Jefferson City's capitol. The lounge of the Legislative Assembly was selected for *A Social History of the State of Missouri*. The mural space is approximately two thousand square feet on three walls, each cut by a door.

For eighteen months, Benton researched. He traveled five hundred miles across Missouri, filling his sketchbooks. He had to find authentic tools, the right mule, a full-blooded

Osage Indian. There are five trains in the mural and 235 portraits. Benton said, "I never put anybody in a picture of this kind unless I have had an opportunity to become acquainted with him or to sketch him from life." The mural was to be the living soul of Missouri, the people and the land.

Benton made detailed pencil and wash studies of anatomical fragments. He designed alternate compositions. It took him two months to construct a clay model fifteen feet long and twenty inches high. From the clay model Benton drew value studies in ink and pencil and did small preliminary color sketches.

The second week of July, 1936, Benton began preparing the walls. He started work at six in the morning and worked steadily until about five in the afternoon. At lunchtime, he munched on cheese and crackers, painting the whole time. Most of July and August the temperature was over one hundred degrees. There were times he had to cool his tubes of paint in a bucket of ice. Six months later the mural was finished.

Many found Benton's style too loud, too disturbing. Walter Heren of *The Kansas City Journal-Post* reported that among the people he polled, "You either like 'em or you want the wall painted a deep black." Shortly before Thomas Hart Benton died, he said, "If I have any right to make judgments,

I would say that the Missouri mural was my best work."

Within a month the controversy had passed. *A Social History of the State of Missouri* is still on the walls of the House Lounge. Thomas Hart Benton was a realist painter who never abandoned the design principles and explosive color of abstract art. He revolutionized public art, making it for and about the people, founding the Regionalist movement. Benton's America was not the America of great men and epic events. Benton's America was everyday people going about their ordinary lives, brilliantly.

Connect the dots:

Edwin Hubble (1889-1954)
Raisins in Rising Bread

The night sky was as familiar to Hubble as your neighborhood is to you. He showed that our galaxy, the Milky Way, is not the whole universe. During long, cold nights, working in isolation, Hubble photographed the far reaches of space. He showed those faint, blurry blobs out there are not masses of luminous gases; they are other galaxies. Those galaxies, like raisins in a rising loaf of bread, are moving away from each other in space.

Edwin Powell Hubble was born November 20, 1889, in Marshfield, Missouri, the third of eight children. His mother's father, Dr. William Henderson James (a distant relative of Jesse James), owned W.H. James and Son Drug Store. Using parts available in his store, Grandfather James built a small telescope. Ed was fascinated.

Ed did not have many friends. His classmates said Ed thought he knew all the answers to everything. So Ed did not want a big party for his eighth birthday. He wanted to stay up all night and watch the stars and moon through his grandfather's telescope. It was cold outside, and there was school in the morning. Ed had to promise that he would bundle up and that he would not be late for school. Wrapped in his fuzzy gray sweater with a cap on his head, earmuffs pulled securely down over his ears, Ed stuffed a gigantic sandwich in his pocket and a couple of cookies. The stars were bright and there was a sliver of moon. Long after his grandfather was asleep, Ed was in the backyard watching the stars revolve through the night sky. He forgot to eat.

Ed loved reading adventure books, especially H. Rider Haggard's *King Solomon's Mines*, Edgar Rice Burroughs' *Tarzan*, and Jules Verne's *Journey to the Centre of the Earth*. Edwin was only sixteen when he entered the University of Chicago. Six feet, five inches tall, handsome and athletic, he fought on the university boxing team as a heavyweight and graduated with a Bachelor of Science in astronomy and physics. He won a Rhodes Scholarship to study for three years at Oxford University in England.

When Edwin returned to the United States, he was reserved and dignified. He spoke with an English accent, sported a pipe, dressed in tweeds, and was an insufferable Anglophile (lover of everything English). He wore knickers (pants that end at the knee) and a signet ring. Eight-year-old Betsy wondered what had happened to her big brother.

Edwin started graduate school at the University of

Chicago's Yerkes Observatory. The Yerkes telescope is a forty-inch refractor, a lens that you look through. It is the largest of its type. The title of Edwin's written doctoral research is *Photographic Investigations of Faint Nebulae*. It was a topic that would become his life's work. Dr. Edwin Hubble took charge of the recently installed one hundred-inch reflecting telescope (a mirror instead of a lens) at the Mount Wilson Observatory near Pasadena, California. Many astronomers thought the Milky Way was the entire universe. It was a mere few hundred thousand light years across. One light year, the distance light travels in a year, is six trillion (6,000,000,000,000) miles.

Dr. Hubble was a careful, tireless researcher. Spending long, cold nights alone at the telescope, he photographed distant nebulae. It turns out that those dim patches of light, Hubble's nebulae, are not clouds of dust; they are clusters of stars. Each nebula is a separate galaxy containing billions of stars, and the galaxies are more or less uniformly distributed across space, a pattern like tennis balls fifty feet apart.

Hubble photographed the depths of space to a distance of more than one hundred million light years, the limit of the one hundred-inch telescope. He found seventy-five million galaxies. Studying photographs of these galaxies, Hubble developed an elegant classification system based on shape. Some galaxies are balls, some flatter, more like eggs, and some are flattened out into a spiral. Our Milky Way is a spiral galaxy.

One of the Milky Way's stars is our sun. Stars burn bright and give off lots of energy. Planets like Earth get heat and light from their star. The star's light tells what it is made of. As light passes through a prism, it bends, forming a rainbow band of colors called a spectrum. The longest waves are red, the shortest, violet. Lots of elements are being burned inside the sun. One of them is hydrogen, another is calcium. Water is two parts hydrogen and one part oxygen. Hydrogen makes one dark line at one end of the sun's spectrum. It is calcium in milk that makes your bones strong. Calcium causes missing wavelengths that show up as two dark lines in the middle of the sun's spectrum.

Light behaves like a wave. It exhibits the Doppler effect. That means as it moves toward the viewer, the waves push against each other, getting shorter. As it moves away, the waves stretch out. With sound, the pitch of a train rises as it approaches, and falls as it rushes away. In the same way, the light waves shorten if galaxies are moving toward us and lengthen if they are moving away. The spectral lines of our neighbor, the Andromeda spiral galaxy, are blueshifted. It is moving toward us. All distant galaxies have redshifted spectral lines. Hubble showed that the more the spectral lines are redshifted, the faster the galaxy is moving away. He found far galaxies racing away at twenty-five thousand miles per second!

There are different types of stars. Galaxies have all the star types, so galaxies are all fairly similar. A galaxy's distance from us is determined by its brightest stars. Hubble showed that the dimmer those stars, the more the spectral lines are redshifted. This led to Hubble's law: The further away the galaxy is, the faster it is traveling away from us. Hubble's law applies to all uniformly expanding objects, like inflating balloons or loaves of bread rising in the oven. It is the visible evidence of the expanding universe.

Since everything in the universe is moving away from everything else at breakneck speed, logically everything was together at some time in the distant past. This led to the idea of the universe originating from a single point with a Big Bang.

Launched April 14, 1990, the Hubble Space Telescope is continuing the famous astronomer's work. Without the interference of Earth's atmosphere, the specialized cameras and spectrograph can see further into space. The further away we look, the further back in time we see. Edwin Hubble would have loved having the magnificent telescope named after him.

❭ Galaxy Pinwheel

Instructions for Galaxy Pinwheel:

1. Color the stars and bands of the galaxy pinwheel.

2. Cut out the square.

3. Cut the four diagonal lines from the corners to the dot at the end of the line.

4. Using a tack or push pin, punch holes at the dots labeled A, B, C, D, and at the center circle.

5. Lift each lettered corner and pull it down so the hole meets the hole at the center.

6. Place your tack down through each hole (white side of the paper), but not through the center hole yet.

7. Put the tack through the center hole together with all the corners.

8. Place a bead on the tack, then push the tack into a stick near one end.

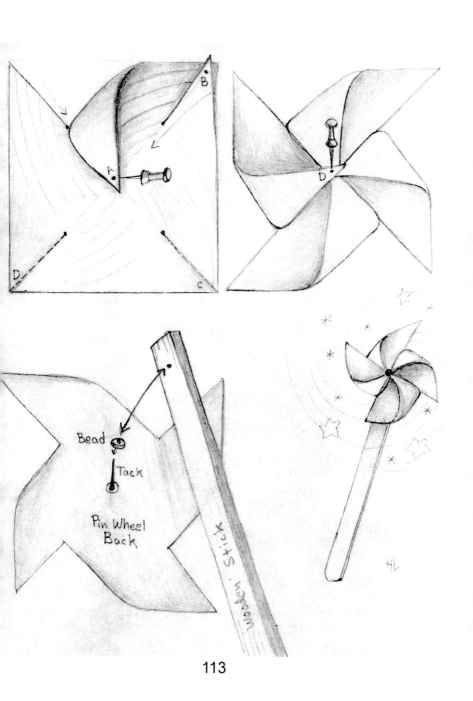

Bead

Tack

Pin Wheel
Back

Wooden Stick

▶ Make your pinwheel.

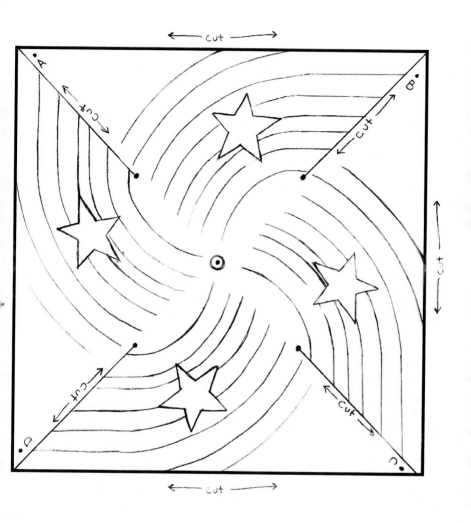

Walt Disney (1901-1966)
The World's Biggest Boy

There is no question Walt Disney was a genius. A kinda, sorta, Midwestern hick, he changed every aspect of the cartoon industry, and then went on to bring a whole new vision to amusement parks.

Walter Elias Disney was born in Chicago, Illinois on December 5, 1901. He had three older brothers and would have a younger sister. When Walt was four years old, the Disneys settled on a farm outside of Marceline, Missouri. As a child, Walt was always light-hearted, always having fun. He was the exact opposite of Elias, his dour, hard-working father. For Walt, the farm was paradise: "With a wide front lawn. Big weeping willow trees. It had two orchards." There were horses and a few cows, pigs, chickens, and ducks. To herd the pigs, Walt climbed on the back of the biggest hog and rode him out to the pond to root. Sometimes the young cowboy got shrugged off into the mud.

Walt's father did not smoke or drink or swear, but he had a violent temper. Flora, Walt's gentle mother, turned the children's bread butter-side-down so Elias wouldn't see that she was "wasting" butter. Butter should be sold. Elias was a hard worker and expected the same from his sons. He often beat them. Eventually the two oldest boys ran away, and Elias got sick. The farm lost money. Five years later, Elias moved the family to Kansas City.

There, Elias bought a one-thousand paper newspaper route. It was Walt's job to deliver fifty newspapers, morning and evening, seven days a week. He was up at 3:30 in the morning. The papers had to be placed under a brick to be sure they didn't blow away, or inside the storm door when it snowed. He had to leave school fifteen minutes early to deliver the evening paper. He was often so tired that he catnapped in an apartment hallway or behind a garbage can in an alley. He did not do well in school.

Bert Hudson's barbershop at Thirty-First Street was on Walt's paper route. Sometimes Walt sat in a chair in front of the shop and drew cartoons. Mr. Hudson liked the cartoons. He offered Walt a free haircut in exchange for them. Later, the barber bought them for ten or fifteen cents. The best part was that Mr. Hudson hung the drawings in the window for everyone to see.

When Walt was eighteen, he and a shy, talented artist with the unlikely name of Ub Iwerks founded a cartoon studio in Kansas City. After a few years, "Iwerks and Disney" went bankrupt. Walt moved to Hollywood and set up a studio in his uncle's garage. His first big success was Oswald the Lucky Rabbit. Walt, always bubbly, did the selling and created the stories. Foolishly, Walt sold the distributor the rights to the Rabbit. Then the distributor hired the animators away from Disney.

Ub Iwerks had followed Walt from Kansas City. The others quit, but Ub stayed on. Together they created Disney's greatest character—Mickey Mouse. Walt, who invented the storyboard (most filmmakers today use a storyboard), came up with storylines, and Ub gave the plucky mouse his familiar form. They were halfway through *Steamboat Willie*, the third Mickey Mouse cartoon, when Walt attended a screening of *The Jazz Singer*, Hollywood's first "talkie." The next morning, *Steamboat Willie* was rewritten for sound. When filming was completed, Walt previewed it at the studio. Wives and friends were invited. Walt's brother Roy, who handled the studio finances, projected the film through a window so the machine's clatter would not interfere with the sound effects. Walt did Mickey's high-pitched voice. Watching the back of the bedsheet screen, the studio animators played a harmonica, shook rattles, struck a xylophone, twirled noisemakers, and banged on spittoons. The six minute cartoon was shown over and over again until everyone had a chance to see it. They loved it.

November 18, 1928, is Mickey Mouse's birthday. That day, *Steamboat Willie* premiered at the Colony Circle in Hollywood. It was the first film to have a perfectly synchronized soundtrack, and it propelled Walt Disney to fame. The Academy of Motion Picture Arts and Sciences awarded Disney a special Oscar. By 1932, there were more than a million Mickey Mouse Clubs in the United States. Two and a half million Mickey Mouse watches were sold the first two years they were available.

Walt and his wife Lillian purchased a new home west of Los Angeles. Always intrigued by trains, Walt built a one-eighth scale steam train on a half-mile track that ran around his property (and under Lillian's flower garden). Days he did not go to work, he put on his striped overalls and conductor's cap. Climbing on the train's tender, Walt drove his two daughters and the neighbor children around on the train. Walt loved pulling its whistle and ringing its bell.

Saturdays Walt took his daughters to amusement parks. But the parks were dirty, and that offended him. Sometimes he took the girls to ride the merry-go-round. He sat on a bench munching popcorn, thinking there should be something for adults to do, too. He decided to design his own clean park. The artists and engineers who designed Disneyland were called "Imagineers." They wrote their ideas on squares of paper and put them up on a board. Afternoons, Walt would go over to the "sandbox," as he called the Disneyland office, and juggle the papers around. To pay for the park, Walt produced a show on America's new hot entertainment—television. The first episode of *Disneyland* was dedicated to a preview of the park with a salute to Mickey Mouse. "I hope we never lose sight of one thing," host Walt Disney said, "...that this was all started by a mouse." It was not long before *Disneyland* became the number one show on television.

Walt hovered over every detail of Disneyland. An acquaintance called it "The world's biggest toy for the world's biggest boy." One of the first attractions completed was a train. Entry was down Main Street, Walt's idealized turn-of-the-century version of Marceline, Missouri. Main Street led to Sleeping Beauty Castle where "guests" could branch off into Adventureland, Frontierland, Fantasyland or Tomorrowland.

Today the Disney Studio is the largest in the world. New Disney theme parks have opened in Paris, Hong Kong, and Tokyo. Walt Disney had a fantastic imagination, and his unassuming little mouse made him famous. He and Mickey just wanted to make people laugh.

▶ Kicking Mule Cartoon

1. Cut out along dashed lines.

2. Tape "B" on top of "A" along left margin to make a hinge.

3. Tightly roll "B" around a pencil, all he way up to the hinge. When you let go the paper will curl.

4. On a table, hold down "A" + "B" along the hinge at the left.

5. View the cartoon by sliding the pencil over the curled paper, unrolling and rolling "B."

6. Watch the mule kick.

Langston Hughes (1902-1967)
The Black Experience

Jim Crow laws were in effect from 1876 to 1965. They established separate public train cars, bus seats, restaurants, restrooms, etc. for black and white people. Missouri's law stated, "It shall be unlawful for any colored child to attend any white school, or any white child to attend a colored school."

Langston Hughes was black. He wrote about blacks, for blacks. During the Harlem Renaissance, a time when black culture was popular with white America, Langston Hughes was the most famous of the black poets. He firmly believed that his words could change America.

Langston Hughes was born February 1, 1902, in Joplin, Missouri. His situation was odd for a black child. His father was a lawyer. Shortly after Langston was born, James Hughes moved to Mexico to escape the color discrimination in the United States. He owned several businesses and a large ranch in Toluca, Mexico. He had a thriving law practice and became a financial success. Sometimes he sent money for Langston, but never for Langston's mother.

Langston's mother was college educated and wanted to be an actress. She was often away looking for work, but when she was home she took Langston to shows and to the movies. From age two to thirteen, Langston mostly lived in Kansas with his struggling grandmother. A college educated widow, she took in laundry.

Langston loved the movies. When he was in the seventh grade he got his first job, a job his grandmother did not approve of. He swept the lobby and scrubbed the halls of an old hotel. He cleaned the toilets and shined the mirrors and spittoons. He was paid fifty cents a week. Langston was thrilled. The movies were fifty cents, so every Saturday he went. He saw Charlie Chaplin and Mary Pickford. He saw Pearl White in *The Iron Claw*.

He had been going to the movies for months. Then one Saturday he was refused a ticket. Mrs. Pattee, the owner, put up a sign: No Colored Admitted. It was difficult for twelve-year-old Langston to understand. Hadn't he been buying movie tickets and sitting in the theater for months? What was different? He wasn't different. Why?

> I swear to my soul
> I can't understand
> Why freedom don't apply
> To the black man.[1]

[1] Langston Hughes, "The Black Man Speaks"

In 1920, eighteen-year-old Langston took a train from Ohio, where his mother was living, to Mexico to ask his father for money for college. As Langston crossed the Mississippi River toward St. Louis at sunset, he took an envelope from his pocket and on the back he wrote one of his most famous poems, "The Negro Speaks of Rivers."

After a year in Mexico, Hughes enrolled at Columbia University in New York. New York's Harlem was the center of black American culture. Hughes was entranced. He quit school after a year, moved into Harlem, and immersed himself in Harlem's vibrant cultural life. The 1920s were the decade of the Harlem Renaissance—of jazz, the Charleston, and books by black authors. Langston's "The Negro Speaks of Rivers" was published in the June 1921 issue of *Crisis*, the magazine of the NAACP (National Association for the Advancement of Colored People).

Langston's grandmother had told him that their ancestors were from Africa. In order to visit the "motherland," Langston found work as a messboy on the S.S. *Malone* sailing to Africa. He would have a chance to meet his black brothers.

In Africa, Langston found a "long, sandy coastline, gleaming in the sun. Palm trees sky-tall. Rivers darkening the sea's edge with the loam of their deltas. People black and beautiful as the night." But Africans did not welcome Langston like a long lost brother. Langston's skin was copper brown and his hair was more straight than curly. He had American Indian and white ancestry as well as African. To the Africans he was white! Langston Hughes was not white in America, where a drop of black blood makes you black, but he was not black in Africa, where a drop of white blood makes you white.

Langston returned to Harlem and published a collection of poetry, *Weary Blues*. A second collection was published the following year, *Fine Clothes for the Jew*. Langston liked his second collection better because it was less personal than *Weary Blues*, more about other people. The book received good reviews from literary magazines and the white press. But dozens of black reviewers didn't like it. Eustace Gay's review appeared in the *Philadelphia Tribune* on February 5, 1927. He wrote, "It does not matter to me whether every poem in the book is true to life.... Our aim ought to be to present to the general public...our higher aims and aspirations, and our better selves." Langston's reply was, "I didn't know the upper class Negroes well enough to write much about them. I knew only the people I had grown up with, and they weren't people whose shoes were always shined.... But they seemed to me good people, too."

> Reach up your hand, dark boy, and take a star.
> Out of the little breath of oblivion
> That is night,
> Take just
> One star.[2]

[2] Langston Hughes, "Stars"

Langston Hughes published sixteen volumes of poetry, ten collections of short stories, two novels, two autobiographies, nine books for children, more than two dozen stage works, numerous articles, films, radio scripts, song lyrics, anthologies, and translations.

My People

The night is beautiful,
So the faces of my people.
The stars are beautiful,
So the eyes of my people.

Beautiful, also, is the sun,
Beautiful, also, are the souls of my people.[3]

[3]Langston Hughes " My People"

▶ **Write your own poem:**

My Poem

_____

_____

_____

_____

_____

_____

Satchel Paige (1906-1982)
A Blazing Fastball

Satchel Paige may have been the greatest pitcher baseball has ever known. But it sure wasn't obvious at the beginning. Born Leroy Robert Paige on July 7, 1906, in Mobile, Alabama, Satchel was the seventh of eleven children in a dirt-poor, black family. His mom was a laundress, his dad a gardener. Bringing home money was more important than going to school.

At age seven, Leroy was toting suitcases (called satchels back then) for people at Mobile's train depot. He earned a dime a bag. He was tall for his age. He got himself a stick and some rope so that he could carry more suitcases and make more money. The other kids laughed and said he looked like a walking satchel tree. The name stuck.

For a while he collected bottles and swept up at Eureka Gardens, the Mobile Tigers' ballpark. He liked baseball and wanted to play. But a baseball cost money, so Satchel threw rocks. He discovered that he had a natural gift. He could hit what he aimed at.

Twelve-year-old Satchel was walking home from a game late one afternoon. His clothes were torn and dirty. It was getting dark as he passed a toy store. "Unless you've gone around with nothing, you don't know how powerful a lure some new, shiny stuff is." Inside, Satchel stuffed a handful of toy rings in his pocket. A big white man collared him at the door. The result is written in a book at the Mobile Courthouse: "On this day, the 24th of July, 1918, Leroy Paige is ordered committed to the Industrial School for Negro Children at Mount Meigs, Alabama."

Reform school was scary at first. But the people were kind, the meals regular, and the clothes warm. The baseball coach taught Satchel to pitch—kick high and block out the sky, let go of the ball when your hand is in the batter's face, read the batter's weaknesses from the movement of his knees.

Until he was eighteen years old and a skinny six feet, three and a half inches tall, Satchel Paige stayed at Mount Meigs. Visitors' day was Satchel's worst day. For five and a half years, no one came to see him.

When Satchel got back to Mobile, he got a job pitching for the semi-pro Tigers at Eureka Gardens. Semi-pro meant a dollar on a good day and a keg of lemonade on a bad day. For two years, Satchel pitched for the Tigers.

It was a crucial game. Satch had a twenty-five game

winning streak going and was looking to be picked up by a professional team. The Tigers were winning 1-0. With two outs in the ninth inning, the Tiger infielders made three errors and loaded the bases! Something had to be done. Satchel called the outfielders to the mound and made them sit down behind him. The crowd stopped booing and started yelling. A fly ball would lose the game. Satch turned and calmly struck out the next batter.

Not long after, Satchel was offered fifty dollars a month to pitch for the Chattanooga Black Lookouts, his first professional job.

St. Louis Cardinals' Dizzy Dean was the biggest name pitcher in the world. Dizzy was white and pitched in the major leagues. Although black and white teams didn't play against each other during the regular season, they did in postseason exhibition games. In 1934 and 1935, Dizzy Dean pitched against Satchel Paige. Satchel won four of the six games. Dizzy was not modest, but he said, "My fastball looks like a change of pace alongside that little pistol bullet old Satchel shoots up to the plate."

Josh Gibson—a barrel-chested black slugger—and Satch were teammates and good friends. Josh was one of the best power hitters ever. He said to Satch, "One day we are going to be on opposing teams and you'll be pitching and I'll come up to bat with the bases filled. I'm going to slam one into left field." Everyone laughed, but ten years later it almost happened.

In the 1942 Negro World Series, Satchel was pitching for the Kansas City Monarchs and Josh was batting for the Homestead Grays. The Monarchs were leading 2-1. There were two outs and a man on base. Satch walked the next two batters, loading the bases, so that he could pitch to Josh. Satch's teammates thought he was nuts. Josh was the most feared hitter in black baseball.

A hush fell over the crowd. Satch said, "I'm going to throw you a fastball letter high." Josh did not move the bat. Strike one. "Now I'm going to throw you another fastball. It'll be a little faster and belt high." Strike two. Everyone was standing, going crazy. "I'm going to throw you another fastball, but it will be even faster than the last one. I'm not going to throw any smoke at your yoke. It'll be a pea at your knee." Strike three. Josh never even moved the bat. Truth was, Satch knew Josh never relaxed when he was pitching to him. Josh couldn't decide if Satch was jivin' him, so he just stood there.

After the regular 1938 season, Satchel was playing winter ball in Mexico when his arm went numb. He could not pitch. J.L. Wilkinson, owner of the Kansas City Monarchs, the best black team in the Midwest, decided to help out. He gave Satch a job playing first base with their traveling team and maybe pitching a few innings. Wilkinson knew Satchel's name would still draw a crowd. Satchel was grateful. After several months, his arm got better. The next season, thirty-three-year-old Satchel Paige pitched the Monarchs to the championship of the Negro League's American Division. And he did it again each of the next three years. Satchel settled in Kansas City, bought a house, married, and had seven children. Kansas City was the first place he called home.

Integration came to baseball in 1947. After twenty-two years as a professional in the black leagues, Satchel Paige joined the Cleveland Indians. At forty-two, he was past his prime and his fastball had slowed. But he had experience. Satchel pitched the Indians to the American League pennant, and they went on to win the World Series. Satchel Paige had reached the pinnacle of baseball.

Dizzy Dean said it best: "That skinny old Satchel Paige with those long arms is my idea of the pitcher with the greatest stuff I ever saw."

▶ Crossword

ACROSS

1. Possibly the greatest pitcher baseball has ever known.
3. Three strikes and you are ___.
5. In the 1942 Negro World Series, who did Satchel play for?
8. In what season do baseball players train?
10. Who was Satchel's friend and rival?
11. What game did Satchel and Josh play?

DOWN

1. The game's winner is determined by the _____.
2. If the batter hits the ball and circles the bases, it is called a _____.
4. Throw.
6. The _____ at Mount Meigs taught Satchel to pitch.
7. When Satchel was twelve years old, he stole a bunch of rings from a _____.
9. A catcher uses a _____ to protect his hand.

◗ Crossword answers

Puzzlemaker Alice Anna Reese

Illustrated by Heinrich Leonhard

Jane Froman (1907-1980)
Crushed Velvet

If there is such a thing as a perfect radio voice, Jane Froman had it. Not only blessed with a beautiful voice, she had a beautiful smile, and was always kind and generous.

Ellen Jane Froman was born at home on November 10, 1907, in University City, a suburb of St. Louis. Her mother, Anna Barcafer Froman, was an accomplished pianist who had studied in Europe. Her father, Elmer Froman, was a traveling salesman. They had been members of a church choir in St. Joseph. Jane's mother wrote in Jane's baby book that at two years, three months, Jane sang five songs, including "I Love You Truly."

Shortly before Jane's fifth birthday, a second child was born. Jane was sent to Clinton, Missouri, to stay with her grandmother and the large, prominent Barcafer family. The baby, Margaret Ann, had spina bifida, a birth defect where the spinal column is not completely covered with bone. Today doctors can fix spina bifida, but they could not in 1912. Jane's parents stayed in St. Louis to be with her. Margaret Ann was in the hospital until she died at age four months.

Family tragedies are hard on marriages. When the baby died, Jane's mother came back to Clinton. Elmer never joined them. Jane loved her jolly, extroverted father. She missed him terribly. She started stuttering then, and she stuttered all her life.

Anna gave piano and voice lessons for one dollar an hour in order to support herself and her daughter. Jane already had a lovely voice. Anna taught her careful breathing and perfect enunciation. Ironically, Jane never stuttered when she sang.

Jane was six when she was put in school at the Holy Rosary Convent. She stuttered, and the children made fun of her. She was miserable. She was also required to spend an hour practicing piano every day. Jane didn't want to practice, didn't need to practice. She could play anything by ear. For spite, she bit the piano from one end to the other, leaving big tooth marks in the wood.

Jane's life got better when Anna was hired as director of voice at Christian College (now Columbia College), and they moved to Columbia, Missouri. It was a prestigious girls' school at the time, both a high school and a two-year college. Anna taught voice, and Jane attended classes.

When Jane graduated, she entered the School of Journalism at the University of Missouri. She did not have any interest in journalism, but the J School put on an annual musical revue. She got the lead in *Bagdaddies*, sang and danced the hit number, "Mystic Moon," was a great success, and flunked out of the university. Her mother, recently married to the mayor of Columbia, was mortified.

In the fall, Jane was "banished" to the Cincinnati School of Music. She was on her own. As a freshman, she got a scholarship intended for seniors. She also gave concerts in private homes. At one of these private performances, a radio producer heard her sing the "St. Louis Blues." He hired her.

Jane started out singing advertising jingles on the radio. Her first job was for Tom's Roasted Peanuts, and it paid ten dollars. She would later joke about starting out "singing for peanuts."

Within a few years, Jane was a celebrity. Her warm, velvet voice was heard on the *Chesterfield Hour*, America's most popular weekly radio program. During Christmas, she starred in a smash hit production of New York's *Ziegfeld Follies*. She pioneered the handheld microphone. Jane Froman was the number one female singer in 1934. "Radio's sweetest songbird" could be heard on seven radio shows every week.

World War II began. In the spring of 1942, Jane gave three War Bond benefit concerts in Columbia. The performances were scheduled at the University of Missouri, Columbia College, and Stephens College. Columbia was segregated at the time. Black Americans were not allowed in the auditoriums. It did not make sense to Jane that young men who were ready to go off and fight for their country could not attend a concert because of their skin color. She rented the auditorium at Douglass High School, hired a band, printed up flyers and programs, and scheduled a fourth concert for black servicemen. She paid for all of it herself. Management was furious. Jane didn't care.

In 1943, at President Roosevelt's request, Jane flew to Europe to entertain the troops. The plane crashed into the Tagus River just outside of Lisbon, Portugal. Jane's right leg was crushed, her left leg nearly severed below the knee. Her right arm had multiple fractures, her pelvis was dislocated, and a couple of ribs were broken. But her face was not touched and her voice was unaffected.

It took two years for the doctors to piece her right leg together. Jane wanted to fulfill her mission to entertain America's brave fighting men. The war was over, Jane's leg was still in a cast, and she was in constant pain. Nevertheless, Jane sailed to Europe to entertain the injured and the homesick. She was immensely popular. The men saw her in a wheelchair or on crutches, triumphing over her disabilities and singing songs of peace and hope and home. They loved her.

After thirty-four years in show business, Jane Froman retired to Columbia, Missouri. She found an old friend from Journalism School, Rowland Haw Smith. Friendship blossomed into love and they were married June 22, 1962.

Jane was always looking for ways to help people. Everyone

loved her. She was a master musician with an extraordinary voice. Twentieth Century Fox made a film about her life, *With a Song in My Heart*. In addition to her years on radio, she made records and acted in films. Hollywood honored her with three stars on its Walk of Fame. Clinton, Missouri, Jane Froman's childhood home, declared her "a symbol of courage and unselfishness."

▶ Jane Froman Paper Doll:

To make Jane sturdy, paste her on cardboard before cutting her out.

Color the paper doll and cut her out.

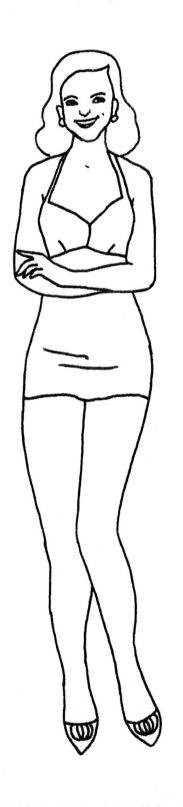

▶ Jane's Uniform:

Color her uniform and cut it out. See how Jane looks in her uniform!

▶ Jane's Gown:

Color her beautiful performance gown and cut it out...

Using your own paper, design more clothes for Jane.

Helen Stephens (1918-1994)
Fulton's Fleetest Feet

Helen Stephens had big feet. She wore size twelve shoes. But those feet could move. In 1936, she won the Olympic title for the 100-meter sprint. In that same competition, Jesse Owens won the men's title. Like Jesse, Helen broke the world record with that race. Owens' record lasted for five years; Stephens' remained unbroken for twenty-four years.

Helen Herring Stephens was born in Fulton, Missouri on February 2, 1918. Her father farmed 240 acres a mile west of Fulton. Helen went to Middle River School, a one room country school with twenty-five students about a mile from the farm. Her classmates called her Hellie. Helen's cousin, Thornton Meloy, rode a horse to school. Helen trotted alongside Thornton holding on to his stirrup. If the horse jumped a ditch, Helen jumped the ditch. If the horse splashed through a stream, Helen splashed through, too. Helen kept pace easily. But Thornton would shake her if he could. Then Hellie raced ahead.

There was a spot in the Stephens' cornfield where nothing grew. It was a saltlick where Indians had hunted deer and where Helen and her little brother often hunted arrowheads. It was a lazy summer day and, as usual, eight-year-old Helen was barefoot and wearing overalls. She lay back, sucking on a stem of grass, a bunch of arrowheads clutched in her hand.

Hellie fell asleep and dreamed she was running. She was the fastest runner in the world. Crowds cheered and applauded madly as she broke the winner's ribbon. She held the silver cup high over her head as thousands roared their approval. Hellie had never heard of the Olympics. She ran back to the house to tell her mom about her great dream. "Go feed the chickens," was her mother's response.

At fifteen, Helen was a tall, gawky country girl, uncomfortable in dresses. Her feet were so big, her shoes had to be custom made. But she could outrun, out jump, out hit the boys in her high school, and she wanted a school letter like the boys. She had to run fifty yards in 7.0 seconds to qualify. She asked Coach W. Burton Moore if she could try. He lined up several girls. Helen was wearing baggy pantaloons and dirty sneakers. She had had no training. The girls raced down the school's cinder driveway. Coach Moore clocked her at 5.8 seconds. "You'll have to do it again," he said. "I didn't get your time." She ran the fifty yards in 5.8 seconds again. It wasn't possible: That time was the current world record!

The coach trained Helen with the boys. They were her biggest fans. In 1935, the girls' national Amateur Athletic Union championships were held at the new St. Louis Arena. Helen had no money, no shoes, no uniform. Coach Moore paid her two dollar entry fee. A Westminster College student, T.J. Neukomm, lent her his spikes. Johnny Lutz, another Westminster student, lent her his sweats. It was 110 miles to St. Louis. Helen rode in Coach Moore's clanky old Ford. Her racing buddies trundled into a second car. They were her cheering section.

Helen said, "Friday, March 22, 1935; it's a date permanently chiseled in my memory." The day was stormy. Four thousand people watched the seventy-five girls and women compete in track and field events. They could hardly wait to see Olympic titleholder Stella Walsh. She was a pro and seven years older than Helen. Helen's first competition was the shot put. She won. Her second competition was the standing broad jump. She won. Her third event was the 50-meter race. No one had ever heard of seventeen-year-old Helen Stephens. Stella Walsh, the Olympic World Champion female sprinter, was also entered. Helen won in 6.6 seconds. The crowd went wild. Coach Moore said Helen had the grace of an antelope and an effortless eight and a half foot stride that combined all of the elements of perfect sprinting form. Her little brother said, "She don't milk the cows no more. Hellie says that's man's work. I hav'ta do it now."

On the day of the 100-meter race at the 1936 Berlin Olympics, it drizzled. Helen was competing in the discus just as the 100-meter event was to begin. Stella Walsh, Helen's only real competition, was already set when Helen streaked across the field. I can do it, Helen told herself, I'll make my dream come true. Gobs of slippery mud clung to her spikes. The track was a gooey mess. Quickly she dug a footing hole. The ball of her foot securely set, the starting gun fired. Her arms and legs pumped like pistons. She ran like the demons of hell were after her. When she broke the winner's ribbon, Stella was two meters behind her. The audience went crazy. Helen had won in 11.5 seconds. She had broken the world record.

As they walked to the podium, the new champion extended her hand to the former champion. It was a gesture of pure sportsmanship on Helen's part. The crowd cheered again. Helen was proud. When the laurel wreath was placed on her head, she thought, someday someone is going to come along and make me look like I was standing still. But it was twenty-four years before Helen's record was broken.

The February 1937 issue of *Look* magazine included an article entitled, "What Do You Think? Is This a Man or a Woman?" Helen sued. *Look* paid up. The next year, Helen took her winnings from the *Look* suit and formed her own basketball team, the Helen Stephens Olympic Co-Eds. She was the first woman to own and manage her own basketball team. For ten years the girls played men's rules against men's teams, laughing, cutting up, and often winning. She took up bowling, and at age twenty-two she was elected president of the Powder Puff bowling league in Berkeley, a suburb of St. Louis. In the 1960s and 1970s she worked on Olympic committees. She was hired as part time coach to form a women's track team at William Woods College, her alma mater. In the 1980s and early 1990s, Helen was a consistent gold medalist in the national Senior Olympics and Missouri Show-Me Games.

Helen Stephens lived her dream. Not only was she the fastest woman in the world, she was a lifetime athlete. She was inducted into seven different halls of fame. She was a major player in the sports world her entire life.

How fast can you find the right track to the winner's circle?

Bibliography

Thomas Hart Benton

Adams, Henry. *Thomas Hart Benton: An American Original*. NY: Alfred A. Knopf, 1989.

Thomas Hart Benton: An American Original. An Exhibition Organized by The Nelson-Atkins Museum of Art. Kansas City MO: Trustees of The Nelson Gallery Foundation, 1989.

Baigell, Matthew. *Thomas Hart Benton*. NY: Abrams, 1975.

Benton, Thomas Hart. *An Artist in America*, 4th rev. ed. Columbia: University of Missouri Press, 1983.

Burroughs, Polly. *Thomas Hart Benton: A Portrait*. Garden City NY: Doubleday, 1981.

Hurt, R. Douglas and Mary K. Dains, eds. *Thomas Hart Benton: Artist, Writer and Intellectual*. Columbia: The State Historical Society of Missouri, 1989.

Priddy, Bob. *Only Rivers are Peaceful: Thomas Hart Benton's Missouri Mural*. Independence MO: Independence Press, Herald Publishing House, 1989.

WEBSITES

http://www.nytimes.com/2003/12/08/arts/painting-to-sound-the-alarm-in-the-wake-of-pearl-harbor.html

Boller Brothers

Ehrlich, George. *Kansas City, Missouri, An Architectural History 1826-1976.* Kansas City MO: Historic Kansas City Foundation, 1979.

Soren, Noelle. "Part III The Missouri Theatre Columbia, Missouri." Art History, University of Missouri, ca. 1975.

—— *Windows to Wonderland: Cinespace Creations of the Boller Brothers, Architects.* Tucson AZ: MGP Publishing, 1999.

INTERVIEWS

Berchek, Marge, at the Missouri Theatre Center for the Arts, Columbia, 2009.

Pollack, Frank, at the Missouri Theater, St. Joseph, 2009.

WEBSITES

Boller Brothers Architectural Records

http://shs.umsystem.edu/kansascity/manuscripts/k0065.pdf

Cinema Treasures / Carl Boller

http://cinematreasures.org/architect/14/

Cinema Treasures / Robert O. Boller

http://cinematreasures.org/architect/15/

Calamity Jane (Martha Canary)

Chartier, JoAnn and Chris Enss. "Calamity Jane: Mysterious Marvel." In *She Wore a Yellow Ribbon: Women Soldiers and Patriots of the Western Frontier*. Guilford CT: Twodot, 2004.

McLaird, James D. *Calamity Jane: The Woman and the Legend*. Norman: University of Oklahoma Press, 2005.

Etulain, Richard W. "Calamity Jane: Independent Woman of the Wild West." In *By Grit & Grace: Eleven Women Who Shaped the American West*. Golden CO: Fulcrum Publishing, 1997.

—— "Calamity Jane: The Making of a Frontier Legend." In *Wild Women of the Old West*. Norman: University of Oklahoma Press, 1992.

CHILDREN'S BOOKS

Faber, Doris. *Calamity Jane: Her Life and Her Legend*. Boston: Houghton Mifflin, 1992.

Krall, Sarah. "Calamity Jane." In *100 Folk Heroes Who Shaped World History*. San Francisco CA: Bluewood Books, 1995.

WEBSITE

www.worldwideschool.org/library/books/hst/biography/LifeAdventuresCalamityJane/Chap1.html

Kit Carson

Carter, Harvey Lewis. *'Dear Old Kit': The Historical Christopher Carson*. Norman: University of Oklahoma Press, 1968.

Roberts, David. *A Newer World*. NY: Simon & Schuster, 2000.

Sides, Hampton. *Blood and Thunder*. NY: Doubleday, 2006.

CHILDREN'S BOOKS

Campion, Nardi Reeder. *Kit Carson, Pathfinder of the West*. Champaign IL: Garrard Publishing, 1963.

Gleiter, Jan and Kathleen Thompson. *Kit Carson*. Milwaukee: Raintree Publishers, 1987.

George Washington Carver

Elliott, Lawrence. *George Washington Carver: The Man Who Overcame*. Englewood Cliffs NJ: Prentice-Hall, 1966.

Kremer, Gary R., ed. *George Washington Carver: In His Own Words*. Columbia: University of Missouri Press, 1987.

CHILDREN'S BOOKS

Adair, Gene. *George Washington Carver*. NY: Chelsea House Publishers, 1989.

Aliki. *A Weed is a Flower: The Life of George Washington Carver*. NY: Simon & Schuster, 1988.

Halvorsen, Lisa. *George Washington Carver: Innovator in Agriculture*. Farmington Hills MI: Blackbirch Press, 2002.

Wheeler, Jill C. *George Washington Carver*. Edina MN: ABDO & Daughters, 2003.

Walt Disney

Eliot, Marc. *Walt Disney: Hollywood's Dark Prince*. NY: Birch Lane Press, 1993.

Gabler, Neal. *Walt Disney: The Triumph of the American Imagination*. NY: Alfred A. Knopf, 2006.

CHILDREN'S BOOKS

Fanning, Jim. *Walt Disney*. NY: Chelsea House Publishers, 1994.

Jaffe, Elizabeth Dana. *Walt Disney*. Milwaukee WI: World Almanac Library, 2001.

Thomas, Bob. *Walt Disney: Magician of the Movies*. NY: Grosset & Dunlap, 1966.

Fisher, Maxine P. *Walt Disney*. NY: Franklin Watts, 1988.

Eugene Field

Below, Ida Comstock. *Eugene Field in His Home*. NY: E.P. Dutton & Co., 1898.

Conrow, Robert. *Field Days: The Life, Times, and Reputation of Eugene Field*. NY: Charles Scribner's Sons, 1974.

Field, Eugene. *Lullabye-land: Songs of Childhood*. Boulder CO: Shambhala, 1979.

State Historical Society of Missouri. Vertical File. "Eugene Field."

Thompson, Slason. *Eugene Field: A Study in Heredity and Contradictions*. NY: Charles Scribner's Sons, 1901.

CHILDREN'S BOOKS

Borland, Kathryn Kilby and Helen Ross Speicher. *Eugene Field, Young Poet*. Indianapolis: Bobbs-Merrill, 1964.

eBOOKS

Field, Eugene. *Love Affairs of a Bibliomaniac*. Charlottesville: University of Virginia Library, 1996.

Jane Froman

Seuling, Barbara. *Say It with Music: The Life and Legacy of Jane Froman*. Princeton IL: Boxing Day Books, 2007.

Stone, Ilene. *Jane Froman: Missouri's First Lady of Song*. Columbia: University of Missouri Press, 2003.

Stone, Ilene and Suzanna Grenz. *One Little Candle: Remembering Jane Froman*. San Diego: Petunia Publishing, 1997.

COLLECTIONS

Columbia College, Columbia MO, Archives. The Jane Froman Papers include notes for Jane Froman's unwritten autobiography, *Time to Go Home*, video of CBS-TV "A Musical Trip to Scotland," *The Jane Froman Show* 1954, and various magazine and newspaper articles.

Western Historical Manuscripts Collection, Columbia MO. The Jane Froman Papers include a biography written by John Burn, Jane Froman's second husband.

MOVIE

With a Song in My Heart Twentieth Century Fox, 1952.

Edwin Hubble

Burroughs, Edgar Rice. *Tarzan of the Apes.* NY: Signet Classics, 2008.

Christianson, Gale E. *Edwin Hubble: Mariner of the Nebulae.* NY: Farrar, Straus and Giraux, 1995.

Haggard, H. Rider. *King Solomon's Mines.* London: Penguin Classics, 2007.

Hubble, Edwin. *The Realm of the Nebulae.* New Haven CT: Yale University Press, 1936.

Sharov, A.S. and Igor Novikov. *Edwin Hubble: The Discoverer of the Big Bang Universe.* Cambridge, England: Cambridge University Press, 1993.

State Historical Society of Missouri, Vertical File "Hubble Family."

Verne, Jules. *Journey to the Centre of the Earth.* London: Puffin Books, 1994.

CHILDREN'S BOOKS

Datnow, Claire L. *Edwin Hubble: Discoverer of Galaxies.* Springfield NJ: Enslow Publishers, 1997.

Fox, Mary Virginia. *Edwin Hubble: American Astronomer.* NY: Franklin Watts, 1997.

Langston Hughes

Bloom, Harold, ed. *Langston Hughes (Bloom's BioCritiques).* Philadelphia PA: Chelsea House Publishers, 2002.

Hughes, Langston. *The Collected Works of Langston Hughes.* Vol. 2, *The Poems: 1941-1950.* Columbia: University of Missouri Press, 2001.

—— Vol. 4, *The Novels: "Not Without Laughter" and "Tambourines to Glory."* Columbia: University of Missouri Press, 2001.

—— Vol. 11, *Works for Children and Young Adults: Poetry, Fiction, and Other Writing.* Columbia: University of Missouri Press, 2003.

—— Vol. 12, *Works for Children and Young Adults: Biographies.* Columbia: University of Missouri Press, 2001.

—— Vol. 13, *Autobiography: "The Big Sea."* Columbia: University of Missouri Press, 2002.

—— Vol. 14, *Autobiography: "I Wonder As I Wander."* Columbia: University of Missouri Press, 2003.

—— Vol. 15, *The Short Stories.* Columbia: University of Missouri Press, 2002.

Rampersad, Arnold. *The Life of Langston Hughes.* Vol. 1. NY: Oxford University Press, 1986.

Tidwell, John Edgar and Cheryl R. Ragar, eds. *Montage of a Dream: The Art and Life of Langston Hughes.* Columbia: University of Missouri Press, 2007.

CHILDREN'S BOOKS

Myers, Elizabeth P. *Langston Hughes: Poet of His People.* Champaign IL: Garrard Publishing, 1970.

Walker, Alice. *Langston Hughes: American Poet.* NY: HarperCollins Publishers, 1974.

WEBSITE

http://en.wikipedia.org/wiki/Jim_Crow_laws

Jesse James

Bruns, Roger A. *Jesse James: Legendary Outlaw.* Springfield NJ: Enslow, 1998.

Croy, Homer. *Jesse James was my Neighbor.* NY: Duell, Sloan and Pierce, 1949.

Edwards, John Newman. *Noted Guerrillas, or, The Warfare of the Border.* Shawnee KS: Two Trails, 1996.

Fellman, Michael. *Inside War: The Guerilla Conflict in Missouri during the American Civil War.* NY: Oxford University Press, 1989.

Keeley, Mary Paxton. *Back in Independence.* Chillicothe MO: Community Press, 1993.

Ross, James R. *I, Jesse James.* Dragon Publishing Corp, 1988.

Settle, William A. *Jesse James was his Name: Or, Fact and Fiction Concerning the Careers of the Notorious James Brothers of Missouri.* Columbia: University of Missouri Press, 1966.

Yeatman, Ted P. *Frank and Jesse James: The Story Behind the Legend.* Nashville TN: Cumberland House, 2000.

FILMS

United Artists. *The Long Riders.* 1980.

Warner Bros. *The Assassination of Jesse James by the Coward Robert Ford.* 2007.

Mary Paxton Keeley

Keeley, Mary Paxton. *Back in Independence*. Chillicothe MO: Community Press, 1993.

—— *Dear Aunt Mary: Selected Writings and Excerpts from Her Letters*. Chillicothe MO: Community Press, 1997.

|Keeley| Mary Paxton. *River Gold*. Indianapolis IN: The Bobbs-Merrill Co., 1928.

—— *The Kettle Singing*. Boston MA: Walter H. Baker Co., 1929.

Keeley, Mary Paxton, ed. *Boone County Cook Book*. Columbia MO: The Service Guild of Calvary Episcopal Church, n.d.

—— *Lyrics from a Linotype*. Columbia MO: Christian College *Microphone*, 1934.

—— *Christian College Prize Plays* Columbia MO: Christian College, 1934.

Paxton, Mary and Henry Lancaster Mueller. *Little Vinnie Ream: A Play in Three Acts*. Performed at Christian College Auditorium, May 18, 19, 20, 1944.

Truman, Margaret. *Bess W. Truman*. NY: Macmillan, 1986.

WEBSITE

www.trumanlibrary.org/hstpaper/keeley.htm

Satchel Paige

Holway, John B. *Josh and Satch: The Life and Times of Josh Gibson and Satchel Paige*. NY: Carroll & Graf, 1991.

Paige, Leroy (Satchel). *Maybe I'll Pitch Forever: A great baseball player tells the hilarious story behind the legend.* Ed. David Lipman. Garden City NY: Doubleday, 1962.

—— *Pitchin' Man.* Ed. Hal Lebovitz. Westport CT: Meckler, 1948.

Ribowsky, Mark. *Don't Look Back: Satchel Paige in the Shadows of Baseball.* NY: Simon & Schuster, 1994.

CHILDREN'S BOOKS

Adler, David A. *Satchel Paige: Don't Look Back.* NY: Harcourt, 2007.

Cline-Ransome, Lesa. *Satchel Paige.* NY: Simon & Schuster, 2000.

Gutman, Dan. *Satch & Me.* NY: HarperCollins, 2006.

Humphrey, Kathryn Long. *Satchel Paige.* NY: Franklin Watts, 1988.

McKissack, Patricia and Fredrick McKissack. *Satchel Paige: The Best Arm in Baseball.* Berkeley Heights NJ: Enslow Publishers, 2002.

Nelson, Kadir. *We Are the Ship: The Story of Negro League Baseball.* NY: Jump at the Sun/Hyperion, 2008.

Paige, Satchel. *Satchel Sez.* David Sterry and Arielle Eckstut, eds. NY: Three Rivers Press, 2001.

Rubin, Robert. *Satchel Paige: All-time Baseball Great.* NY: G.P. Putnam's Sons, 1974.

Schmidt, Julie. *Satchel Paige.* NY: The Rosen Publishing Group, 2002.

Sturm, James and Rich Tommaso. *Satchel Paige: Striking Out Jim Crow.* NY: Jump at the Sun/Hyperion, 2007.

James Cash Penney

Beasley, Norman. *Main Street Merchant: The Story of the J. C. Penney Company*. NY: Whittlesey House, McGraw-Hill Book Company, 1948.

Brown, John W. *Missouri Legends: Famous People from the Show Me State*. St. Louis MO: Reedy Press, 2008.

Penney, James Cash. *Fifty Years with the Golden Rule*. NY: Harper & Brothers, Publishers, 1950.

—— *Lines of a Layman*. Great Neck NY: Channel Press, 1956.

—— *The Man with a Thousand Partners: An Autobiography of J.C. Penney as told to Robert W. Bruere*. NY: Harper & Brothers, Publishers, 1931.

—— *View from the Ninth Decade: Jottings from a Merchant's Daybook*. NY: Thomas Nelson & Sons, 1960.

CHILDREN'S BOOKS

Hudson, Wilma J. *J.C. Penney: Golden Rule Boy*. NY: The Bobbs-Merrill, Company, 1972.

WEBSITE

http://www.hoovers.com/j.-c.-penney/--ID__10810--/free-co-profile.xhtml

Sacred Sun

Calloway, Colin G. *One Vast Winter Count: The Native American West before Lewis and Clark*. Lincoln: University of Nebraska Press, 2003.

Cosentino, Andrew F. *The Paintings of Charles Bird King (1785-1862).* Washington D.C.: Smithsonian Institution Press, 1977.

Ellis, Richard N. and Charlie R. Steen, eds., "An Indian Delegation in France, 1725," *Journal of the Illinois State Historical Society* 67 (1974): 385-405.

Ewers, John C. "Charles Bird King, Painter of Indian Visitors to the Nation's Capital" *Smithsonian Institution Annual Report 1953.* Washington D.C.: Smithsonian Institution Press, (1854) 463-473.

Fletcher, Alice C. "The Osage Indians in France." *American Anthropologist* 2 no. 2, 1900.

Foreman, Carolyn Thomas. "Curiosity on the Continent." *Indians Abroad, 1493-1938.* Norman: University of Oklahoma Press, 1943.

Foreman, Grant. "Our Indian Ambassadors to Europe," *Missouri Historical Society Collections* 5 no. 2, 1928.

Josephy, Jr., Alvin M. (ed.) *Lewis and Clark through Indian Eyes.* NY: Alfred A. Knopf, 2006.

Mathews, John Joseph. *The Osages: Children of the Middle Waters.* Norman: University of Oklahoma Press, 1961.

McKenney, Thomas L. and James Hall. "Mohongo (An Osage Woman)" *The Indian Tribes of North America,* vol. 1. Edinburgh: John Grant, 1933.

McMillen, Margot Ford. "Les Indiens Osages: French Publicity for the Traveling Osage" *Missouri Historical Review* 97, no. 4, 2003.

McMillen, Margot Ford and Heather Roberson. "Sacred Sun," *Into the Spotlight: Four Missouri Women*. Columbia: University of Missouri Press, 2004.

[Peter C. Marzio] Perfect Likenesses: Portraits for History of the Indian Tribes of North America (1837-44). Catalogue for an exhibition April-September 1977 National Museum of History and Technology, Smithsonian Institution, Washington D.C.

Rollings, Willard H. *The Osage: An Ethnohistorical Study of Hegemony on the Prairie-Plains*. Columbia: University of Missouri Press, 1992.

Shoemaker, Floyd C., ed. "Missouriana–Mohongo's Story" *Missouri Historical Review* 36, no. 2, 1942.

Viola, Herman J. *The Indian Legacy of Charles Bird King*. Washington D.C.: Smithsonian Institution Press and Doubleday & Company, 1976.

Wied-Neuwied, Maximillian Alexander Philipp, Prinz von. *People of the First Man: Life Among the Plains Indians in Their Final Days of Glory*. NY: E.P. Dutton & Co, 1976.

Wolferman, Kristie C. *The Osage in Missouri*. Columbia: University of Missouri Press, 1997.

Wood, W. Raymond. *Prologue to Lewis and Clark: The Mackay and Evans Expedition*. Norman: University of Oklahoma Press, 2003.

WEBSITES

The Osage Indians

www.uark.edu/depts/contact/osage

The Osage Tribe's Official Homepage

www.osagetribe.com

First People/Treaties

http://www.firstpeople.us/FP-Html-Treaties/TreatyWithTheOsage1825.html

Malachite's Big Hole

www.mman.us/chardonfrancis.htm

State Historical Society of Missouri

http://shs.umsystem.edu/historicmissourians/name/s/sacredsun/

CHILDREN'S BOOK

Riehecky, Janet. *The Osage*. Mankato MN: Bridgestone Books, 2003.

Belle Starr

Bausch, Richard. "The Man Who Knew Belle Starr" *Scribner Anthology of Contemporary Short Fiction*. NY: Simon & Schuster, 1999.

Camp, Deborah. *Belle Starr: A Novel of the Old West*. NY: Harmony Books, 1987.

Morgan, Speer. *Belle Starr: A Novel*. Boston MA: Little, Brown and Company, 1979.

Shirley, Glenn. *Belle Starr and Her Times: The Literature, The Facts, and The Legends*. Norman: University of Oklahoma Press, 1982.

CHILDREN'S BOOKS

Green, R. Carl and William R. Sanford. *Belle Starr*. Hillside NJ: Enslow Publishers, 1992.

Walker, Paul Robert. *Belle Starr: A Lady Among Outlaws*. In

Great Figures of the Wild West. NY: Facts on File, 1993.

MAGAZINES

"Morgan hopes for a rising Starr." In *Mosaics*. University of Missouri, College of Arts and Science, 2008.

DVD

The History Channel. *Wild Women. The Best of the Real West*. NY: Greystone Communications, 1992.

Helen Stephens

Hanson, Sharon Kinney. *The Life of Helen Stephens: The Fulton Flash*. Carbondale: Southern Illinois University Press, 2004.

Herren, Laura. "Gold metalist 'flashes' back." In *Rural Missouri*. August 1983.

State Historical Society of Missouri. Vertical File. "Helen Stephens."

Stephens, Helen (1918-1994). Papers. Western Manuscript collection.

Harry S Truman

Ferrell, Robert H., ed. *The Autobiography of Harry S Truman*. Boulder: Colorado Associated University Press, 1980.

Gies, Joseph. *Harry S Truman: A Pictorial Biography*. Garden City NY: Doubleday & Co., 1968.

Harry S Truman Presidential Museum and Library. Tammy Kelly, archivist.

McCullough, David. *Truman*. NY: Simon & Schuster, 1992.

State Historical Society of Missouri. Vertical File. Harry S Truman [Atomic Bomb].

Thomson, David S. *A Pictorial Biography HST: The Story of Harry S. Truman, 33rd President of the United States*. NY: Grosset & Dunlap, 1973.

Truman, Margaret. *Bess W. Truman*. NY: Macmillan Publishing, 1986.

Mark Twain

Kaplan, Fred. *The Singular Mark Twain: A Biography*. NY: Doubleday, 2003.

Meltzer, Milton. *Mark Twain Himself: A Pictorial Biography*. NY: Bonanza Books, 1960.

Priddy, Bob. *Across Our Wide Missouri*. Independence MO: Independence Press, 1994.

Twain, Mark. *The Adventures of Tom Sawyer*. Mineola NY: Dover Publications, 1998.

—— *The American Claimant; Pudd'nhead Wilson*. Garden City NY: Nelson Doubleday, n.d.

—— *The Autobiography of Mark Twain*. Charles Neider, ed. NY: Harper Perennial, 1990.

—— *A Connecticut Yankee in King Arthur's Court*. NY: Barnes & Noble, Inc., 1995.

—— *The Diaries of Adam and Eve*. Amherst NY: Prometheus, 2000.

—— *How Nancy Jackson Married Kate Wilson and Other Tales of Rebellious Girls & Daring Young Women*. Lincoln: University of Nebraska Press, 2001.

—— *The Innocents Abroad*. NY: Signet Classics, 2007.

—— *Life on the Mississippi*. Mineola NY: Dover Publications, 2000.

—— *A Murder, A Mystery, and A Marriage*. NY: W.W. Norton, 2001.

—— *Personal Recollections of Joan of Arc*. Garden City NY: Nelson Doubleday, n.d.

—— *The Prince and the Pauper and Other Stories*. NY: Dodd, Mead & Co., 1965.

—— *Roughing It*. Hartford CT.: American Publishing Co., 1872.

—— *A Tramp Abroad*. NY: Hippocrene Books, 1982.

Twain, Mark & Charles Dudley Warner. *The Gilded Age*. Garden City NY: Nelson Doubleday, n.d.

COMPACT DISCS

Holbrook, Hal. *Mark Twain Tonight!* Sony BMG Music Entertainment, 2006.

Laura Ingalls Wilder

Anderson, William. *Laura Ingalls Wilder Country*. NY: HarperCollins, 1990.

Hines, Stephen. *I Remember Laura: Laura Ingalls Wilder*. Nashville: Thomas Nelson, Inc., 1994.

Miller, John E. *Becoming Laura Ingalls Wilder: The Woman Behind the Legend*. Columbia: University of Missouri Press, 1998.

Spaeth, Janet. *Laura Ingalls Wilder*. Boston: Twayne, 1987.

Wilder, Laura Ingalls. *By the Shores of Silver Lake*. NY: Harper & Row, 1939.

—— *The First Four Years*. NY: Harper Trophy, 1971.

—— *Little House in the Big Woods*. NY: Harper & Row, 1932.

—— *Little House in the Ozarks: The Rediscovered Writings*. Stephen W. Hines, ed. NY: Galahad Books, 1991.

—— *Little House on the Prairie*. NY: Harper & Row, 1934.

—— *Little Town on the Prairie*. NY: Harper & Row, 1941.

—— *The Long Winter*. NY: Harper & Row, 1940.

—— *On the Banks of Plum Creek*. NY: Harper & Row, 1937.

—— *On the Way Home: The Diary of a Trip from South Dakota to Mansfield, Missouri in 1894 with a setting by Rose Wilder Lane*. NY: Harper & Row, 1962.

—— *These Happy Golden Years*. NY: Harper & Row, 1943.

—— *West From Home: Letters of Laura Ingalls Wilder San Francisco 1915*. NY: HarperCollins, 1974.

Wilder, Laura Ingalls and Rose Wilder Lane. *A Little House Sampler*. Edited by William T. Anderson. NY: Harper & Row, 1988.

Zochert, Donald. *Laura: The Life of Laura Ingalls Wilder*. NY: Avon Books 1976.

MICROFILM

Wilder, Laura Ingalls. "Pioneer Girl." Wilder's handwritten draft of her unpublished autobiography, written in 1930. State Historical Society of Missouri in Columbia. Microfilm.

Contributors

Alice Anna Reese has a B.A. in English and a Ph.D. in Animal Science. She was a member of Prince Edward Island's Writers' Guild as well as a founder and ten year member of P.E.I.'s writing and publishing cooperative, TWiG, The Writers in Group. She is a graduate of the Institute of Children's Literature. Currently, she writes with Write/Hear, Columbia's chapter of the Society of Children's Book Writers and Illustrators, and is a member of the Columbia, Missouri Freelance Forum and the local chapter of the Writers' Guild. She won First Place in the Essay Division of Callaway County's One Hundred Years Writing Contest. Recently, her writing appeared in the Columbia Art League's show Interpretations and is published in its accompanying book.

Heinrich Leonhard was born in Tubingen, Germany in 1955. His family immigrated to the United States when he was a small child. They settled in Missouri in 1960. Heinrich graduated from the University of Missouri with a B.S. in Geology. While at the University, he studied painting under

Frank Stack. Heinrich has been a self-employed ceramic artist since 1982. http://hleonhard.com He created a ceramic ornament for the White House Christmas Tree in 2001. He worked with Grant Elementary School in Columbia, Missouri to create a tiled bench in 2007. On November 13, 2008, the Missouri History Mural was unveiled at the Columbia Public Library. Heinrich worked with the 2007-2008 fourth grade class at Grant Elementary School to create the mural, which is located near the children's area. Heinrich is not only interested in the prehistory of Missouri, but the more recent history as well. He is treasurer of the Boonslick Chapter of the Missouri Archaeological Society.

Aimee Leonhard was born in Los Angeles, California and moved to Missouri to attend college. She studied drawing at Hollywood High School and Stephens College, as well as in Paris. She earned a B.A. and an M.A. in Art History from the University of Missouri. She worked at the Museum of Art and Archaeology on the University campus as Assistant Art Conservator until 2000. She works at the Columbia Public Library as a Library Associate and as Art Archivist for the library. She has collaborated on several projects with her husband, Heinrich Leonhard.

CPSIA information can be obtained
at www.ICGtesting.com
Printed in the USA
FFOW01n2318130616
24948FF

9 781936 688500